Awakening
blackout girl

A Survivor's Guide for Healing from

Addiction and Sexual Trauma

by

JENNIFER STORM, MA

With a Foreword by Kristen Schmidt, MD
Hazelden Betty Ford Foundation

Hazelden
Publishing

Hazelden Publishing
Center City, Minnesota 55012
hazelden.org/bookstore

Printed in the United States of America

Library of Congress Cataloging-in-Publication Data

Storm, Jennifer, 1975- author.

Awakening blackout girl : a survivor's guide for healing from addiction and sexual
trauma / Jennifer Storm.

Center City : Hazelden Publishing, 2020. | Includes bibliographical references.

LCCN 2020022091 (print) | LCCN 2020022092 (ebook) | ISBN 9781616499037
(trade paperback) | ISBN 9781616499044 (ebook)

LCSH: Resilience (Personality trait)—Juvenile literature. | Sexual abuse—Juvenile
literature. | Substance abuse—Juvenile literature.

LCC BF723.R46 S67 2020 (print) | LCC BF723.R46 (ebook) | DDC 362.76/4—dc23

LC record available at https://lccn.loc.gov/2020022091
LC ebook record available at https://lccn.loc.gov/2020022092

Editor's notes:
This publication is not intended as a substitute for the advice of health care
professionals.

Readers should be aware that websites listed in this work may have changed or
disappeared between when this work was written and when it is read.

Alcoholics Anonymous and AA are registered trademarks of Alcoholics Anonymous
World Services.

Hazelden Publishing offers a variety of information on addiction and related areas.
The views and interpretations expressed herein are those of the author and are neither
endorsed nor approved by AA or any Twelve Step organization.

24 23 22 21 20   1 2 3 4 5 6

Cover design: Theresa Jaeger Gedig
Interior design: Terri Kinne
Typesetter: Jessica Ess, Hillspring Books
Developmental editor: Heather Silsbee
Editorial project manager: Betty Christiansen

The biggest threat is a girl with a book.

—Madame Gandhi, "The Future Is Female"

Contents

Foreword by Kristen Schmidt, MD   ix

Introduction   xi

1 Trauma   1

2 Coping with the Effects of Trauma   19

3 Honesty   35

4 Shame   49

5 Humility and Vulnerability   69

6 Self-Harm versus Self-Worth   89

7 Love and Relationships   101

8 Sex   121

9 Grief   141

10 The Survivor Connection   157

11 Setback or Feedback   173

Resources   183

Notes   193

Acknowledgments   197

About the Author   199

Foreword

SLEEP IS A DEFENSELESS STATE. No one understands the truth of this more than those who have been sexually traumatized. In an attempt to avoid recurring nightmares and subvert intrusive flashbacks, many females with trauma histories turn to alcohol and benzodiazepines; many develop substance use disorders as a result. While males account for the majority of misused medications in our country, this is not true for the category of sedatives.[1] There are several psychological and physiological barriers to vulnerability after surviving sexual violence. A blackout is the stuff of such barriers. *Awakening Blackout Girl* by Jennifer Storm goes beyond simply breaking barriers down; it's about doing the more difficult and sustaining work of building something better in its place.

A blackout is a primitive and powerful survival mechanism. It can precede sleep onset to protect our respiratory drive from continued consumption of central nervous system depressants (alcohol, Xanax, heroin). Blackouts can also function to preserve our psychological drives, our ability to think and exist while surviving the unthinkable, in the case of sexual trauma. The author reminds us that the survival mode is a natural response to an unnatural occurrence; the situational must not become sustainable. There is a danger in surrendering to detachment from conscious work that is inherent in Storm's call to action of "awakening" the girl from blackout. She argues for recovery through engagement and examination, acknowledging that self-awareness is her greatest tool.

Dissociation is symptomatic of surviving sexual trauma. Storm writes on page 124, "It becomes easier for us to detach from our bodies and surrender our ownership or autonomy than it is to try to reclaim it." Through a series of exercises and meditations, Storm empowers her readers in an active process of self-discovery. This allows for the development of a healthy sense of autonomy and reattachment to the self and the world. Ultimately, these tools can be used to cultivate the much-needed space for intimacy and connection.

Accessing vulnerability involves work and choice. Storm suggests, "I can put up emotional walls like a talented mason." Yet she acknowledges that addiction is only one form of concrete. For those struggling with trauma, sobriety is not a singular solution. Storm compassionately confronts the limitations of present addiction treatment for addressing violent pasts. She notes, "But there was a huge step missing for those of us with histories of victimization: how do we process the wrongs *others* had committed against *us*?" The question is not rhetorical. Consistent with her theory that love is an action, Storm answers her own question through the act of this book's loving and courageous creation—an extraordinary gift for our patients.

Kristen Schmidt, MD
Hazelden Betty Ford Foundation

Dr. Kristen Schmidt is a board-certified addiction psychiatrist at the Hazelden Betty Ford Foundation who uses—and advocates for—a trauma-informed approach to addiction treatment that takes into account the different ways patients experience the symptoms of trauma.

Introduction

IN THE YEARS SINCE I PUBLISHED my first book, *Blackout Girl*, I have been in total awe of the number of people whom my story has touched in some way. I have received hundreds of emails from people expressing gratitude for how my story has helped them heal. There is no greater gift than to receive such accolades, especially because writing *Blackout Girl* was an effort to share my story with those who need to hear it most and to continue my personal healing process. With this book, I want to go further. I want to share all I have learned on my recovery journey so far and, most important, how you too can awaken to a life beyond your wildest dreams. I'll tell you what has helped me so you can find what will help you. Why am I qualified to offer you advice? As you'll discover, I'm far from perfect. But I have been where you are. I have struggled and made mistakes, and I have ultimately managed to find an incredibly fulfilling life of healing and advocacy. I want you to have that too.

I was raped for the first time when I was twelve years old and then twice more as a teenager. Those experiences, combined with other personal and family traumas, led me to turn to alcohol, marijuana, and eventually crack in an attempt to escape my life and my feelings. Throughout my teenage and young adult years, I attempted to find control in self-harm, disordered eating, and partying until I blacked out. I had so much pain dwelling inside me that I, consciously and subconsciously, decided that it was much better to stay in denial, blacked out, asleep, and unaware of my surroundings than to even consider looking into that darkness. Then, in 1997, I watched my mother die after a long battle with cancer. By that time, I thought I had become a master packer of my emotions—I kept all of my victimization and trauma locked securely inside the places I built for them. But my mother's death was one traumatic experience too many. My emotions spilled out in the form of a brutal suicide attempt.

When I woke up in the hospital the next day, I finally realized I needed serious help. The doctors recommended inpatient addiction treatment, and I agreed to go. The treatment center I went to was amazing, and I learned so much from the staff and the other women there. At the same time, it was not trauma informed. During my intake, they asked if I had ever been sexually assaulted, and I answered yes. That answer meant I was immediately assigned to the all-women's unit—nothing more and nothing less. I guess back then, being a survivor of sexual violence just meant you couldn't be around anyone of a different gender. That felt odd to me at the time, but I had much bigger issues to contend with and didn't have the energy to really question the decision. I just wanted to stay alive another day.

It wasn't until I spent a night listening to a speaker who had successfully completed the program that the reality of my situation hit me. If I wanted to really recover and avoid ever reaching that horribly dark emotional place again, I had a lot of work to do. In her sharing that night, the speaker said, "My secrets keep me sick." I didn't know it yet, but this is a common saying in Twelve Step programs and for good reason. The truth of it hit me like a ton of bricks. I had walked into rehab with countless secrets. Things that had happened to me, truths I had known but couldn't share, thoughts that were so dark I couldn't imagine ever speaking them aloud. Every time something bad happened, I would compartmentalize it inside my mind, body, and spirit. Each secret, each dark and painful experience, had its own proper place, and I kept them all under lock and key. But that night after my mother's death, I learned that there is only so much room in one person to contain that kind of suffering. When I heard that woman say her secrets kept her sick, I intuitively realized that if I was going to be successful, to really live a full and happy life free from my addictions and free from the desire to constantly harm myself, I was going to have to dive deep into these secrets and unlock doors inside of me that had been sealed off for a very long time. I was going to have to look at and process the worst moments of my life.

There wasn't a method for this work within the walls of my treatment center. There were plenty of exercises to help process the wrongs we had committed in our addictions, and we talked a lot about making amends and being accountable. This is all very important work in any type of recovery. But there was a huge step missing for those of us with histories of victimization: how do we process the wrongs *others* had committed against *us*? We never dove deep into the actual sources of our pain.

I believe that everyone's addictions have a root or a source. For me, I can trace the start of my alcohol and drug use to my first assault when I was twelve. I used drugs and alcohol to escape a pain greater than my body, mind, and spirit could process, and that use led me to more pain and more trauma. This pattern developed into a destructive cycle. Something bad happened,

I felt pain, I couldn't deal, so I used, and so on and so on. It was a self-fulfilling prophecy. Maybe you can already identify one event that triggered the start of your cycle of addiction and trauma. Or maybe the source is more insidious than that. For many of us, it was not one event but a slow, consistent buildup of pain over time that led to an increased desire to escape. Abuse, mental and physical health issues, family dysfunction, marginalization, oppression, subjugation, financial hardship, grief . . . the list of potential sources of trauma and addiction is, unfortunately, long.

That stay in rehab marked the beginning of my recovery process, but it wasn't nearly enough. For those of us suffering from both addiction and sexual trauma, regardless of which came first, we cannot treat only the addiction. After rehab, I started attending Twelve Step meetings, which have been amazingly helpful for me. They help keep the fire of my addiction at bay. But I realized that I could not just layer addiction treatment, Twelve Step meetings, and sponsorship over that degree of pain. I had to systematically and simultaneously deal with the pain and trauma that was boiling underneath the addiction. If I didn't address my trauma head-on, I would just be putting a Band-Aid over a bullet hole. I would be continuing to ignore and cover up the root problem. A Band-Aid will hold for a while—it may get you through many days of picking up chips and celebrating a newfound life in recovery. But if the kindling of trauma is still slowly burning underneath it all, that Band-Aid will eventually fly off and lead to a relapse, which could be deadly.

This is why many people find themselves relapsing after years and years of solid addiction recovery. I remember listening to Mackenzie Phillips talk at an addiction conference. She spoke about how she finally managed to get some solid clean time under her belt after struggling for years with her addiction. She became a pillar of her recovery community for over a decade, and then her father died. If you know about her history, you know her father sexually abused her for a large portion of her life. His death reopened a gaping spiritual, emotional, and psychological wound that had been festering beneath the Band-Aid of her recovery. The foundation for her life in recovery was well constructed, but it had a serious underlying flaw. She had never dealt head-on with her past childhood abuse. So she relapsed hard. It wasn't until she found a treatment facility that identified this issue and helped her work through it that she really found true, sustainable recovery. She now serves as an advocate for recovery from addiction and sexual trauma. She has written books about her experiences and travels the world spreading a message of strength and hope. Her story is the perfect illustration of how untreated wounds in recovery can lead to devastating relapses. She was lucky; she survived. So many out there struggling with these demons are not lucky, and their relapse means a life ended.

My fundamental belief about addiction recovery is this: to obtain long-term, sustainable recovery, we must get to the bottom of what motivates us to use. Why do we feel the need to punish ourselves? What are we running away from? What is the underlying feeling? Is there one traumatic event in our history that led us to want to drink or use or harm ourselves? Was it numerous events? A long history of abuse, harassment, hardship, or marginalization? What is that thing that makes us want to pick up our drug of choice even when everything seems to be going well? If left untreated, that thing could destroy everything for us.

When I finally got a glimpse of some real clean and sober time, I started to wake up. In my newly sober state, I started having to look at the things I had avoided for many years. All my wounds were there, like old movies ready to play repeatedly in my head. I could process some of them with my sponsor and Twelve Step group, but in many instances, my pains were so dark and deep that I needed additional therapeutic help. Some things in my history I could not speak about in my addiction recovery meetings because it wouldn't have been appropriate. And, quite frankly, speaking in such a vulnerable group about my history of sexual trauma without first processing it with a professional could have further injured myself or others in my group. Twelve Step meetings are a safe and amazing place to help release the desire to drink or use and to find collective support to not turn to the things that harm us. But they are not the place for deep-rooted therapeutic discovery. Dealing with trauma and victimization is best left in the hands of professionals who can walk us safely through our past experiences so that we can get to the very root of the *why*. If we know the *why*, then we can fully treat it and be free from the core reasons we use.

Once I realized that not only the rape but every other trauma and victimization that came before and after it were my *why*, it was clear to me what I had to do to extinguish that kindling for good. I had to start unpacking myself, my feelings, the traumatic events in my past, and the facts about myself that caused me to feel shame. I could do this only with the help of a trauma-informed therapist. My therapist knew when to push me and when to allow me to be gentle on myself. She had years of experience dealing with trauma and was trained specifically on how to assist me on this journey in a way that would not do more harm or force me so close to the edge that I would fail and use. It has taken me years to do this, but the very understanding that I needed to do it was enough to keep me moving down a path that led to freedom from addiction.

Working on strengthening my coping mechanisms and releasing all those demons tightly stored inside my heart, mind, and soul gave me more freedom than I could have ever imagined. Each time I released some of the darkness inside me, I made room for the light, for the freedom of a new life and a better understanding of myself. That self-awareness has been one of my strongest tools in recovery.

I don't do this recovery thing perfectly every day. Trust me. I am human, and I make mistakes. What's different today is that there isn't any kindling burning underneath my foundation anymore. My recovery foundation is solid and strong. I built it myself, and I know every inch of it. So now, when something traumatizing happens in my life—because, let's face it, life on life's terms brings hardships as well as joys—I don't have to deal with those old layers of trauma anymore. I am able to focus solely on the issue before me, and I have the tools to deal with it in a healthy way.

This is my hope for you. I want you to find this freedom in your recovery. I want you to awaken to a version of yourself that has been waiting for you, just beyond the threshold of the pain. You have to be willing and able to walk through that pain. Trust me, I have tried all the other ways of healing—walking around, jumping over, avoiding—but it was only when I walked *through* the pain, the experience, and the hurt that I truly found freedom from it all. We do not get over things. We get through them.

I want to help you build a rock-solid foundation so when life throws you off balance, you will have plenty of supports to lean on. You can use this book as one tool to guide you in that process. Throughout this book, you will be asked to explore your trauma and your healing process in several different ways. Doing this type of writing and self-exploration can be hard. It can conjure up feelings you may have not experienced in a very long time—or ever. Please make sure to deploy safe coping mechanisms. If you don't already have a trauma-informed therapist, it might be a good idea to find one before you start the exercises in this book. If you find that you're having difficulty processing the feelings brought up by this book, or if you feel you are in danger of returning to unhealthy coping behaviors, take a self-care break. Set up an extra session with your therapist, meditate, share your new feelings with a trusted friend, do some stretching, go for a brisk walk, do fifteen jumping jacks, take ten deep breaths, blast your favorite song and sing at the top of your lungs, or do something else you know will help release your feelings in a safe way. If you don't have a trusted person to talk to and are feeling overwhelmed, please consider calling a victim services hotline or crisis hotline to talk through your response with a trained counselor.

Many of the examples and perspectives in this book come from more than twenty years of experience working in the victim advocacy field, where I support crime victims as they navigate their way through the various justice systems. I have had the privilege of working with a diverse group of victims, survivors, warriors, and thrivers with stories very similar to and very different from my own. Some of the tools and examples included here may be very helpful to you. Others you may not find useful at all. As we say in my Twelve Step groups, take what you need and leave the rest. Let me also take a minute to address the language and terms I'll use in this book. *Sexual violence* is an umbrella term that refers to all unwanted sexual acts, including single or repeated acts of sexual assault, rape, long-term sexual abuse or incest, and others. *Sexual trauma* is the trauma that results from any and all types of sexual violence. I also refer to myself and others as both a *victim* and a *survivor* of sexual violence. Everyone identifies differently. I have used terms like *warrior, thriver,* and many others. Choose what feels right for you. When referring to my addiction, I use the terms *addict* and *alcoholic* because this is how I have identified for a long time. I know not everyone likes or embraces all of these terms and for valid reasons. Please know that when I use these terms and others, I aim to be as inclusive as possible—to reduce stigma, not promote it. Describing what each of us has experienced is difficult, to say the least. Feel free to mentally replace unwanted terms with whatever words you feel best describe you and your circumstances. I see you, you are valid, and I want to include you.

I bring to this book all the knowledge I've gained through my experience as a victim's rights expert, a survivor, an advocate, and a person in long-term recovery. But I'm not a clinician, and this book is not meant to be a clinical guide to treatment of trauma and addiction. My primary qualification for writing this book is that my life is proof that recovery is possible. I'm a survivor of sexual trauma and long-term addiction. And today, I am not just surviving—I'm thriving. I have a rewarding job where I am able to help people like my teenage self every day. I have an incredible wife and son and so many blessings to live for. I was able to achieve all this because I was lucky. After that final suicide attempt, I intuitively knew what support I needed and had the ability to find it. Not everyone is that lucky. This book is my way of paying it forward to everyone who hasn't had the same fortune so far. I don't want you to have to start from ground zero in your recovery process. I will let you know what worked for me and what has worked for the many other survivors I have had the opportunity to meet, so you can figure out what works for you.

I recommend you read this book in chunks, one chapter at a time, so that you can take the time to process the information presented, really work on the exercises, and reflect on the meditation and mantra that end each chapter. If you decide to read multiple chapters in one sitting, I strongly encourage you to revisit each chapter and give yourself plenty of time to fully complete the exercises. I recommend getting a new blank notebook and keeping it beside you as you read. You can use your notebook to answer the questions in the exercises and to jot down any notes or thoughts that occur to you as you're reading. It can be incredibly helpful to go back through your notes at a later time when you're in a different headspace or bring your notebook to your next meeting with your sponsor or therapist. Several of the steps I recommend in the exercises have been truly life changing for me, and that may be true for you as well.

This book is meant to be a journey, not a destination. You should arrive in a different place at the conclusion of it, but you may find that you have more questions than answers. Like me at my moment of realization in rehab in 1997, you may be frustrated to learn that you have much more work to do on yourself than you ever thought—and that's okay. Processing traumatic experiences and learning to recover from them is a process that takes time. And the shape or form of that process may look different for you each day. Above all, be gentle with yourself, and give yourself the time necessary to deal and heal. There is no set time frame for healing. Your unique process is dependent upon your own willingness, desire, and ability to allow yourself to experience, feel, and heal in a way that is safe for *you*. Never let anyone dictate the course you should be on or set a deadline for your personal growth.

My story is proof that there is hope; there is a place beyond the pain. This place is born from the pain but is not owned or defined by it. That is healing. That is hope. The awakening you deserve is available to you. That is the reality waiting for all survivors—for you. Not your pain, nor your offender, nor anyone else who doubts your strength gets to finish your story. *You* have the power to write your ending. *You* can grow through it and become everything you have ever dreamed of and more. I wish you well on your journey of healing growth.

With much love and respect,
Jennifer Storm

If you are having thoughts of suicide, call the
National Suicide Prevention Lifeline at 800-273-8255,
or text with someone on the Crisis Text Line
by texting HOME to 741741.

If you need to talk with someone about being raped
or sexually abused, call RAINN's National Sexual
Assault Hotline at 800-656-4673.

Awakening

blackout girl

Trauma

I had to sit there and relive that strange night. It only came to me in bits and pieces that I didn't ever want to recall, as my lawyer gently tried to pull details from my absent mind. I wasn't really there. I heard noises all around me: the quiet consultation of this man and his lawyer and the questions my lawyer asked. I sensed my parents' dull silence, but I was above it all as though floating in a protective bubble.

—BLACKOUT GIRL, PAGE 18

TRAUMA IS A NORMAL RESULT of experiencing an abnormal event. We may have experienced many very abnormal, traumatic events in our lives. In particular, we may have experienced some form of sexual violence. I think we can all agree that rape, sexual assault, and sexual abuse should be considered very abnormal events—despite how common and normalized these experiences have become in our world. In the United States, a person is sexually assaulted every seventy-three seconds.[2] One out of every five American women (21.3 percent) and 2.6 percent of American men have experienced an attempted or completed rape in their lifetime.[3] No matter how much our society tries to normalize this, it is *not* normal for the human body, mind, or spirit to undergo such trauma.

Those of us who keep track of these statistics know that widespread sexual violence is by no means a new problem—we've seen rates this high, or higher, for as long as we've been keeping records of this data. However, a decade ago, it was very rare to hear the stories behind these statistics, see the faces of the victims, and hear their truth. Today, we are constantly hearing, seeing, and experiencing the traumatic impact of sexual violence in our society. You can't open your social media feeds or turn on the news without hearing about another horrifying case. The constant barrage of news about traumatic events is assaulting in its own right, especially for those of us who have experienced similar events ourselves. The fact that this national health epidemic is finally being acknowledged is vital for educating the public about the importance of preventing these crimes. Telling their stories publicly can also be very healing for some who are speaking out. We as a society want and need to keep hearing these stories. But we also have to understand the impact it is having on all of us—survivors and allies alike.

While sharing our stories can be healing for many of us, it can also be incredibly retraumatizing. It is dangerous to expect anyone to reveal and relive some of the most horrible moments of their lives without also ensuring that these survivors, as well as everyone listening to their stories, have access to adequate, effective, and affordable trauma-informed treatment, therapy, and victim services. Unfortunately, we often see quite the opposite.

• • •

In 2011, a few years into my work as a victim advocate, I worked on the Jerry Sandusky case. That year, a Pennsylvania grand jury report unmasked Sandusky, a once-celebrated Penn State football coach, as the vile predator that he truly is. Pages upon pages detailed the heinous acts he committed on young boys for decades. It was the stuff of nightmares. Many brave young men came forward and spoke their truths, exposing their darkest hours. While our attorney general's office did a phenomenal job of putting a solid case together, it failed in one core area. It had no victim advocates working with these young men. Once the police learned about the abuse, investigators began showing up at the doors of possible victims, asking probing questions about their experiences with Sandusky. Most responded by saying, "I want a lawyer." Later, these young men would be shamed significantly for asking for their legal right to representation. In fact, it became part of the defense's case in trying to dismantle the credibility of these brave survivors. In reality, they were just doing what most people would do, what the media tells us everyone should do if the police start asking questions about our pasts.

It's important to understand that, at the time these officers were knocking at their doors, none of these men knew how widespread Sandusky's abuse was. The silence, shame, and secrecy Sandusky imposed on them led each of the men to believe he was the only victim. Many of them had never told anyone about the abuse they endured, and they had no desire to relive it. Most of them immediately denied the abuse to the police, slammed the door shut, and called an attorney out of fear and self-preservation. Then the reporters came knocking, and it became obvious that something bigger was happening.

All of these young men came from homes with significant poverty and family turmoil. Most did not have a positive male role model or any father figure whatsoever. Then they became interested in football, and a famous and highly respected college football coach started taking an interest in them. He started taking them to games, bringing them onto the field to meet their sports heroes, taking them into the team locker rooms, and buying them football gear and other items that their own families could never have afforded. Sandusky did all this while telling the boys how special they were, how important they were, how loved they were. Trust was built, respect and admiration flooded their young minds, and they looked up to Sandusky as a god. As a savior and, for many, as the father they never had.

Then, slowly and strategically, Sandusky introduced the abuse. One man recalled it starting with Sandusky's hand on his knee while they were driving. He said it did feel odd at first, but he overlooked it because he trusted Sandusky. Eventually, Sandusky's hugs would get just a bit longer. When wrestling and playing, he would tickle them lower on the body, just brushing their private parts. These were all small tests as Sandusky was grooming them. For these children, these were confusing moments. But then it would stop, and they were off to the next amazing experience, the next toy or meal or trip. The boys loved and admired him. So when the grooming evolved into direct sexual abuse, no matter how uncomfortable the boys felt, most of them continued their contact with Sandusky. They were scared and confused. They feared what would happen if someone found out. They feared for Sandusky, for their families, for Penn State football, and for themselves. And they relied on him for so many of their emotional and physical needs at this point—they were scared of what would happen if those good things went away. They were so young. The victims we know of ranged from seven to thirteen years old at the time of Sandusky's abuse. Many of them had never been taught anything about sexual contact—good, bad, or indifferent. Their young brains could not process what was happening to them or figure out what to do in response.

This is the reality for most child victims of sexual assault, a reality that the general public often does not understand.

According to the Department of Justice, 93 percent of perpetrators of child sexual abuse are related to or known to the victim.[4] This prior relationship further confuses victims and increases the shame, fear, and silence that come from these horrific crimes. It is very common for perpetrators to tell their victims that bad things will happen to them, to their friends, and to their family if they tell anyone what is happening. Victims are told that the abuse is a secret, that they are bad, that no one will believe them, that they will lose everyone and everything they love if they make the wrong move. So they endure the abuse and try their best to focus on the good parts of the relationship. And then, when they do finally come forward, or when a police investigator comes knocking on their door many years later, our societal and institutional responses often only further their trauma.

As a society, we are improving these systems and responses. But we still have a long way to go. Victims of sexual violence are often offered little to no support to help them navigate the criminal justice process. There is also still very little recognition of how a victim's trauma might affect the way they respond to the process itself. In the Sandusky case, the only assistance these victims received was from their attorneys. Attorneys are a vital resource for every person involved in the justice system, whether a victim or a perpetrator. But law school does not prepare attorneys to emotionally support traumatized victims. That's not their job. An attorney's job is to explain the criminal justice system to their client and use their knowledge of the law to represent the client in the best way possible. In the Sandusky case, many of the victims' attorneys openly admitted that they had no clue how to deal with the emotional and psychological effects many of these young men were experiencing. Thankfully, two of these attorneys knew me well and called to ask for help for their clients. All of a sudden, reminders of these victims' worst experiences were all over the news and all around their communities. It brought up a tidal wave of trauma that crashed all over their lives. Many of them, with no therapeutic support at all, were drowning.

I'm telling you about these victims because their reactions to their abuse as children, and the way that they were treated by the media and the criminal justice system as adults, reveal a lot of difficult yet common truths about the aftermath of sexual violence. We will unpack these truths throughout this book. But if we want to heal from our trauma, the first step is to understand what trauma is and how it manifests in our lives.

• • •

Let's begin by looking at the immediate chemical and biological responses to a traumatic experience. A traumatic experience can be any event or long-term situation that creates an overwhelming amount of stress. Each person is different, so the same event may be traumatic to one person and cause only temporary stress in another. But sexual violence of any kind is often incredibly traumatic for the survivor.

Most people think they know how they would respond if they were attacked. Most of us say, "I would scream; I would fight; I would run!" Most of us want to believe that we would fly into superhero mode and avoid being harmed—that we would have the ability to protect ourselves. In reality, this is rarely the case.

Let's be very clear here: not all sexual assault or abuse involves violent force. Some rapes happen with very little noise, very little additional physical violence. The actual assault, the act of one intruding upon another's body sexually, is violent in and of itself, no matter the size or strength or relationship of the victim and the perpetrator. A sexual assault is one of the single most violent acts a human can experience. There need not be additional force, bruising, or physical harm done to the victim. Many times, the sheer force of a perpetrator's body mass on top of the victim's is pressure enough to render a victim unable to fight, unable to scream, unable to move. Sometimes, as with the young victims in the Sandusky case, the perpetrator's emotional manipulation prevents the victim from even considering screaming or running as an option.

Yet the absence of visible signs of an attack—like a black eye or a bloody wound—leaves people with the misperception that the victim is okay or at least has not been harmed as much as if they were injured physically. This is a common misnomer in our society and one of the biggest forms of victim blaming and misunderstanding. Trauma leaves invisible wounds. The wounds are emotional and psychological, and if people could be shown the scans that illustrate trauma's impact on the brain, they would see the very real harm done.

We often talk about our biological response to a threat or stressor as our fight-or-flight response. Because we discuss response to threats in this limited way, we all naturally assume that most of us will either run away from a threat or stand our ground and fight. These are in fact possible responses, but this way of thinking leaves out other more common and very normal responses. The focus on fight and flight as the only valid responses has contributed to a culture of victim blaming and shaming and the internalization of that guilt, shame, and humiliation by victims who feel they didn't respond to a traumatic event in the "correct" way. So, let's look at all of the possible responses a victim might have and why no response is more correct or valid than another.

Let's break down your brain to explain what happens in moments of a threat or traumatic experience. You can think of your brain as a very powerful computer. It powers our bodies, stores memories, and determines how we react to specific events, including traumatic ones.

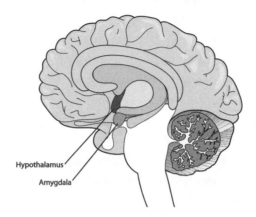

Hypothalamus
Amygdala

Let's start with the amygdala. The *amygdala* is a small, almond-shaped structure located deep in the middle of the temporal lobe. The amygdala receives information from our sensory organs (such as our eyes and ears) and helps to emotionally process that information. The amygdala is designed to detect and interpret threats around us and communicate that information to the *hypothalamus*. When the hypothalamus receives the amygdala's message that there is an active threat, it activates the fight-or-flight response. Think about a time when you were presented with fear or perceived danger. Most likely, your senses became heightened. You may have felt your heart racing or breath quickening. You may have felt suddenly more alert. That response is due to the hypothalamus activating the automatic nervous system, which controls many of the involuntary functions of the body. Part of the automatic nervous system is the sympathetic nervous system, which is what tells the body to produce more adrenaline and speed up these processes. In essence, when a distressing situation is detected, the brain interprets getting rid of that threat as the absolute top priority. Areas of the brain that are focused on more methodical, logical tasks are overridden until the threat is gone.

Psychologist Daniel Goleman talks about this process in his 1995 book, *Emotional Intelligence: Why It Can Matter More Than IQ*. He coined the term *amygdala hijack* to describe our brain's primal function to protect us against threats and danger. When we are in a situation that the amygdala interprets as very dangerous, the more rational parts of our brain get overridden, or hijacked, by stress hormones. These hormones act as stimulants in your body—they may trigger a rush of blood sugar to fill your body to give you more energy; the pupils in your eyes may dilate to enhance your sight; and your blood flow can rapidly increase to allow for increased muscle capacity and speed. Even your airways relax so you can take in more oxygen. Physical symptoms can be the heart racing, sweating, goosebumps, rapid breathing, blurred vision, and more.

These stress hormones are the same chemicals that are released by athletes when competing—they prepare the athletes' bodies for the competition ahead and allow them to perform at maximum capacity. Most of us are not trained athletes, and we do not possess the skills necessary to harness these hormones for productivity. We have not trained for rape or other extreme traumatic experiences the way a runner trains for a marathon. Therefore, these biological responses leave us feeling completely overwhelmed. This is not to say that a trained athlete would necessarily know how to respond to a dangerous threat any differently than a nonathlete.

A rape is very different from a marathon. Just because someone is used to experiencing rushes of adrenaline and cortisol and can control them in one environment does not mean they could do the same when presented with a dangerous threat.

In addition to fight or flight, there is a third kind of response to a threat that we don't talk about nearly as much: freezing. Freezing is another completely normal way our brain and body respond to a fearful or threatening experience. And, in my experience, it is much more common among victims of sexual violence than fighting or fleeing. Think of the commonly used simile of feeling like "a deer in headlights." Almost everyone has had that dream where they are paralyzed by fear, when they try to move and they cannot, or they try to open their mouth and scream, but nothing comes out. This is a very common response to sexual assault. Victims become immobilized and so fearful of what's happening and what else could happen that their bodies and minds freeze. They cannot move; they cannot talk or scream or punch or run. Although it may seem counterintuitive, this reaction can also be our body's way of trying to protect us. Sometimes our brains and bodies decide that, in a specific circumstance, it's not a good idea to try to fight or flee. Sometimes trying to fight or flee could put us in even more danger.

If you've seen any news reporting or responses on social media about stories of sexual violence, you've likely noticed that it's very easy for people to create space between themselves and the victim in the case by asserting how they think they would respond in a similar situation. How often have you heard someone say things like this in response to a news story about an assault?

- "Oh, I would have never gone into that situation."
- "I would have screamed so loudly—why didn't they scream?"
- "I would have fought—no way would I just let someone do that to me."
- "That response doesn't make sense. There must be more to that story."

These are the types of statements we hear all the time from everyday people about allegations of rape and sexual assault. This blame game puts distance between these observers and the victim in the case by portraying a false narrative that *they* are somehow immune to such a crime. That rape or sexual assault couldn't possibly happen to them because they would scream, fight, kick, yell, run. It creates a false sense of safety for that person, and it perpetuates an inaccurate portrayal of traumatic response for whomever happens to be listening. These statements and assumptions are what lead to victim blaming and shaming.

As horrible as it can be for victims to see these kinds of comments in the news or on their social media feeds, they can be even more dangerous than that. A victim-blaming mindset creeps into the minds of jurors and even attorneys, judges, and police officers who haven't been properly trained on how wrong these ideas are. Misinformed assumptions on how a person *would* or *should* act when faced with sexual assault puts into question every single action, or lack of action, on the side of the victim. This is how cases of sexual violence become all about the victim and not the perpetrator. How often do you hear people say things like this in response to a news story about sexual violence?

- "Well, I would never have taken a woman into a back alley and raped her."
- "I would never have forced myself onto an intoxicated person."
- "I would have accepted no as an answer and stopped pushing that person to have sex with me."

Probably never. Comments like this, which rightfully place the blame on the offender and their actions, are unfortunately far less common.

• • •

Let's also touch on another major factor in a very large number of sexual assaults: intoxication or inebriation. We hear a lot about the dangers of "date rape" drugs such as Rohypnol (roofies) and MDMA (ecstasy). These drugs do exist and are very dangerous. We also need to acknowledge that alcohol remains the most common drug used to facilitate sexual assault. Encouraging a person to drink alcohol is easy; it's cheap, it's accessible, and it's cunning. Drinking alcohol is considered so normal in social situations that a perpetrator can often easily convince someone to start drinking, or drink more than they originally planned, without raising any suspicion. When I was raped—not once, not twice, but three times in my life—every assault involved alcohol. This is, unfortunately, true for far too many victims. We often talk about alcohol being a factor in rapes on college campuses, but my assaults happened way before college age. When I was twelve years old, a man more than twice my age plied me with alcohol and got me so intoxicated that I lost consciousness, and he raped me. When I was fifteen, I had only had a couple of drinks and was still alert—my rapist was also drinking when he raped me. I tried to fight, but he was far too big for my five-foot-three,

115-pound body. When I was seventeen, I was passed out from drinking when a thirtysomething scumbag raped me.

We most often hear about alcohol-related sexual assaults happening during college because we have far more data on these assaults. In college cases, at least 50 percent of sexual assaults involve alcohol, and 90 percent of those assaults will be committed by someone known to the victim.[5] But we cannot assume that middle school and high school students are immune to this risk. As long as young people have access to alcohol, as many of them do, there will be an increased risk of sexual assault.

. . .

Traumatic events and situations also greatly affect our memories. Traumatic memories are stored differently within our brains than nontraumatic memories. We can often easily recall an experience that created an emotion and then tie it to what that means for us. For example, going to the beach is a strong sensory experience for me that also connects to emotions. The smell of the salty sea brings forth an energy that surges through my body; the sound of the rushing waves crashing upon the shore is deeply relaxing and comforting to me, and the sight of the never-ending vastness of the ocean conjures my curiosity. For me, going to the beach is a good and safe memory. When I recall these sensory images, I am able to reason that the beach is my happy place. It offers peace and solace, and my intellectual reasoning allows me to understand that the beach is a valued and important place for me. With a good memory, you can fully grasp how you felt and what happened, and you can talk about the good memory without interruption or confusion. It exists in your memory in a chronological way. It is linear. It started this way . . . and ended this way. It simply flows, as do the connections in your brain that record and store the good memory.

Conversely, when a traumatic experience such as sexual violence happens, it adversely affects the parts of our brain that process memory. The part of the brain called the hippocampus is responsible for capturing events in our short-term memory and "encoding" them in our long-term memory. During a traumatic experience like a sexual assault, the sharp increase in stress hormones we talked about earlier can make the hippocampus highly reactive. This is why some parts of a traumatic event, perhaps the moments that we most wish to forget, can feel forever trapped in our brain and recur in the form of flashbacks and intrusive thoughts. However, when we are in a state that is hyperfocused on what we interpret as the most pressing aspect of the experience—whether it be the perpetrator, or a weapon, or the color of a car—we may completely ignore other aspects. We may not be able to recall all of the details of who, what, when, and where the event occurred, because they were never encoded in our brains in the first place.

What's left in our brains in the aftermath of these events are scattered pieces of the experience. This is why most victims of sexual violence cannot recall basic pieces of their own story. It's why, when I was a twelve-year-old victim of rape on the stand at trial, I could not recall the specifics of what happened to me. I felt plenty of emotions connected to the experience, including anger, shame, guilt, and fear, but I could not reason or rationalize why I was feeling this way. Other times, I could wade through pieces of what happened, but I couldn't feel the feelings. I would tell the facts in an almost disconnected and robotic manner, like I was telling someone else's experience. People thought I seemed cold, and I would have inappropriate reactions like laughter at serious moments. These are all very normal responses to extremely abnormal experiences. Our brains are incredibly complex and powerful machines that appreciate the need to protect and conceal in order for a person to survive the unthinkable.

Most traumatic memory reveals itself in spurts. It comes forward through senses like smell, touch, sound, sight, or taste. When a traumatic memory surfaces in the brain, it can bring forth all the same feelings and sensory experiences as the incident that created the memory in the first place. We call these *triggers*. Triggers are things that enable a traumatic memory or force a traumatic memory to the front of our minds. They often come to the surface quickly and throw us completely off balance. Your specific trauma triggers may never go away. I still deal with mine to this day. But I will tell you that you can learn to deal with them appropriately, so that they have much less control over your life. That is part of the important work we will do together throughout this book.

• • •

If you take away only one thing from this chapter, I hope it's this: the way you respond to a threat, a crime, or a violent act is beyond your control. Your brain is biologically wired to respond to threats in a certain way, and there is very little you can do to alter that initial reaction. When you are confronted with an abnormal and dangerous event, your body is hijacked by chemicals that affect everything from your initial response, to your memories of the act, to your ability to cope and manage the stress of the event for months and years to come. While we do know some of the common ways our brains respond to threats, there really are no "normal" or "abnormal" responses. Your individual response to a traumatic experience will depend on your specific brain chemistry as well as all of your background and experiences up to the moment of the threat.

There are common responses to sexual assaults, and everyone's response is unique. Even though it may seem contradictory, both of these statements are true. The next chapter will dive deeper into the long-term impacts of trauma on our brains, bodies, and lives. In that discussion, this same principle remains true: while there are some common reactions that many survivors of sexual violence share, every person is unique. I'll make this clear: no matter how you responded to the traumatic events in your life, no matter how much you were criticized for what you did or did not do in a specific situation, the violence perpetrated against you was not your fault. *You are not to blame.*

We'll talk about and process this much more in later chapters. For now, I encourage you to try these exercises.

EXERCISE 1

Pause for a moment and try to recall a memory that brings forth happiness or peace for you. In your notebook, write down whatever comes to mind as you recall this experience. What do you see? What do you smell? What do you hear? What do you taste? Finally, how do you feel when recalling this memory? Can you write about the memory in a way that tells a story? After writing about the memory, think and write about the internal process you went through. Was it easy to write? Did the images and feelings conjure quickly, or was it difficult to remember certain parts of the experience? Write down any other thoughts you have.

EXERCISE 2

Pause for a moment and try to recall a traumatic memory—an event where you felt fearful or were hurt. If you don't feel ready for this right now, pause and return to this exercise when you're in a better place, or do it in the company of your therapist or a trusted friend. The goal is to begin to explore your memories in a safe way, without pushing yourself too far. In your notebook, write down what comes to mind as you recall this experience. What do you see? What do you smell? What do you hear? What do you taste? Can you write about the memory in a way that tells a story? After writing about the memory, think and write about the internal process you went through. How does recalling this memory make you feel? Was it easy to write? Did the images and feelings conjure quickly, or was it difficult to remember certain parts of the experience? Write down any other thoughts you have.

EXERCISE 3

For the next week, observe how you respond to things that happen in your day-to-day life. Notice if there are any feelings or activities that bring forth memories for you. If so, take the time to write about each of them. Whether you think they are related to your trauma or not, write down the memories and what seemed to trigger them. Try to dissect those experiences to the best of your ability. Answer the same questions about these memories as you did in the previous two exercises. Did this chapter and what you learned change the way you see your experiences? If so, in what way? Elaborate on what you learned and if any of your thoughts or feelings have shifted as a result of this new knowledge.

Meditation

Today, I will forgive myself for any judgment that I may have held against myself for the way I responded to the harm I suffered. I affirm that I was not in control of the harm that came to me. My body, my mind, and my soul responded in the only way they knew how. I am strong. I am human.

Mantra

My response to trauma is mine and mine alone. I will release any judgment I may have about how I responded to the harm that came into my life. My mind, body, and spirit survived in the best way they could. I will no longer beat myself up over my reactions or responses to trauma.

Coping with the Effects of Trauma

All the emptiness in my stomach, that big, black, tight hole,
unraveled and I felt the bliss of emptiness, of nothingness.
This drug did everything I had always wanted alcohol and
other drugs to do—it took away all the pain and left me with
peace. I immediately wanted more. In that instant, crack
became my best friend. I was addicted before I even exhaled.

—BLACKOUT GIRL, PAGE 109

IN THE LAST CHAPTER, we talked about what happens in our minds and bodies when we are presented with a threat or a traumatic event. Now, let's look at the longer-term effects of trauma. Trauma leaves horrific destruction in its wake. And if we're not taught healthy, productive ways to respond to the horrible things that happen to us, we may turn to coping mechanisms that ultimately make us feel even worse.

Before we dig in to the ways we respond to and cope with the aftermath of a traumatic event or situation, let me reiterate a couple of the takeaways from the previous chapter. First, remember that everyone responds to traumatic experiences differently. In this guide, I'm specifically focusing on the trauma experienced in the aftermath of sexual violence. While there are common reactions many of us have, there is no strict process that every single survivor will experience. Second, I want to repeat this: *However you responded to the traumatic situations in your past is valid, it is okay, and you are not alone. Your response was yours, and it was the right response.* This is very important to remember because how we view our initial trauma reactions can impact our thoughts and behaviors for years to come. So please, put down the stick that you have been beating yourself up with over your own response or lack of response to your experience. You do not deserve that type of abuse; no one does.

So what are some common long-term physical, emotional, and psychological effects for survivors of sexual violence? Let's start with physical effects. Not all sexual violence leaves a physical mark, but sometimes it does. The many possible physical effects of different types of sexual violence include vaginal or anal tearing or bleeding, body aches, headaches, chronic pain, trouble walking, cuts, scratches, bruises, scars, broken bones, torn or sprained muscles, sexually transmitted diseases, and pregnancy. Some of these effects heal or resolve over time. Some can be medically treated. Other physical injuries and conditions can last a lifetime for survivors. Fatigue, headaches, body aches, and other chronic conditions can recur throughout a survivor's lifetime and require frequent treatment or medication. Oftentimes, deep emotional and psychological injuries can manifest themselves physically. These are all normal effects when a person's body experiences a highly abnormal intrusion.

I highly recommend seeking medical care after an assault. You may not think you have any physical injuries, but you can't be sure unless you have seen a qualified medical professional. Medical care after an assault is also important for the preservation of evidence for a criminal case. Whether or not you think you will want to press charges against your perpetrator, it's a good idea to have the evidence preserved just in case. If you can, go to a rape crisis center, a child advocacy center, or your local Planned Parenthood for an exam after an assault. The professionals at these clinics are well trained in the effects of trauma and will ensure your confidentiality is maintained. Seeking medical care does not mean that you have to disclose the assault to anyone else, including the police. Your doctor should keep whatever you tell them private unless you give them permission to disclose to someone else.

If you don't have one of these specialty centers nearby, you should go to a hospital or general practitioner's office and insist on seeing a sexual assault nurse examiner, which is a type of forensic nurse specially trained to work with victims of sexual assault. These professionals will know your legal rights and know the proper way to speak to and examine someone who has just had a traumatic experience. Also, request—if not demand—a victim advocate or crisis counselor to be with you through the entire visit. An advocate or counselor should be made available at no cost to you.

Why am I telling you all this? I realize that you may have already gone through the process of seeking professional help for an assault. The sexual violence you experienced may have taken place months or years ago, and you may not have had access to medical care at that time. Or maybe you reported your crime to police or to a medical professional and did not have a good experience. I did not, either. My mother took me to the hospital after I was raped at age twelve. I was not provided an advocate or counselor to help me through the process. I don't have good memories of the doctor who treated me. I was alone, scared, confused, and retraumatized. If your experience was similar to mine, I am so sorry for what you went through. The way so many of us have been treated in the aftermath of violence is incredibly unfair. I do believe our systems for supporting victims are improving, but not fast enough. There are still far too many victims out there today who will take the brave step to report the crime that was done to them and then be retraumatized or revictimized by inadequate or insensitive responses.

That's why I wanted to talk about this. I want to let you know that, no matter how professionals have responded to you in the past, there are well-trained, well-meaning doctors, counselors, therapists, and advocates out there who understand and want to help you. If you were abused or assaulted many years ago and have physical symptoms that you think may be related to sexual violence, it's not too late to get help. If you don't want to speak about your sexual violence history with your doctor, contact your local rape crisis center or one of the national organizations included at the back of this book to learn about your options. I also want you to know how the process of seeking medical care after an assault *should* work. Now, you and anyone you know can feel empowered to ask for what you need and deserve.

Next, let's turn to the emotional and psychological effects of trauma. Every person reacts to sexual trauma in a different way, but there are common symptoms that many of us share. These effects include depression, fear, anxiety, flashbacks, insomnia, nightmares, bed-wetting, shame, guilt, suicidal thoughts, and more. These are all common effects of being violated. Our unique cluster of symptoms is influenced by a mixture of the biological chemicals in our brains and bodies, our emotional states, and our past experiences. The most important things to remember are that all of these symptoms are reasonable and common reactions to experiencing completely abnormal events, and they are outside of our control.

After we go through something traumatic and these physical, emotional, and psychological symptoms begin to manifest, we look for ways to cope. Unless we have an excellent support system at the ready, we will first try to avoid and deny our experience. We push away anyone or anything that reminds us of the experience, and our brains find ways to protect us from the emotional pain. We may learn the art of detachment so we can move through daily life without being truly present. This allows us to avoid the constant intrusion of thoughts about the violence enacted on us. But no matter how many times we push the trauma away, it still simmers beneath the surface, begging to be revealed. It still comes up, and we must find other ways to manage it. In the absence of visible, accessible, low-cost support services and resources, survivors find other ways to cope. We may cope by overeating, harming or cutting ourselves, drinking in excess, abusing prescription medications, taking street drugs, engaging in high-risk sexual behaviors, and more. We turn to these behaviors because they all seem to offer some relief in the moment, but we eventually realize that they are harming us more than they help.

Since you're reading this book, chances are one of your primary unhealthy coping behaviors is the same as mine: substance use. There's no doubt that there is an important connection between trauma, substance use, and addiction. Research has shown that somewhere between 60 and 90 percent of people in the United States who go to treatment for a substance use disorder have experienced at least one traumatic event.[6] And people who have been sexually assaulted are more likely to use marijuana, cocaine, and other major drugs than the general public.[7] Sexual violence survivors often use alcohol, benzodiazepines (benzos), opioids, or other substances in an attempt to cope with their trauma. In a recent Pennsylvania *Patriot-News* report of the sentencing of a horrific rape in Harrisburg, the victim said in her victim impact statement statement that, at first, "she didn't know how to deal with it and lashed out at family members, then tried stifling her feelings by drinking."[8] This is a common progression in the aftermath of sexual violence.

In a way, turning to alcohol in the wake of the extreme stress of sexual violence makes sense. In our society, we treat alcohol as a tool for stress reduction. We are bombarded with images of alcohol that portray it as both an important part of social activities and a way to relax and unwind after a hectic day. Women are particularly targeted with messages that alcohol is the solution to all stressors. The baby boomer generation grew up with ads for bubble bath that said "Calgon, take me away!" Today, ads call alcohol "mommy juice," and greeting cards tell us "It's wine o'clock!" Drinking is treated as a joke, but these messages are promoting a coping mechanism that can become exceedingly dangerous.

Some women are finally speaking out about this, many of whom have fallen prey to the "joke" and then watched as it developed into a substance use disorder. Not funny. In an article called "How Mommy Drinking Culture Has Normalized Alcoholism for Women in America," writer Sarah Cottrell says, "The normalization of mommy wino culture memes and endless parade of articles on mom sites that shouted out the benefits of drinking helped justify my own growing problem."[9] It makes sense that this same culture has spoken to people suffering from the trauma of sexual violence. These positive messages about alcohol seem to offer us a way to cope with our deep pain on a silver platter. It usually takes a long time, and a lot more pain, to fully realize how wrong these messages are.

The way media outlets and advertisers speak about alcohol is one major contributor to the popularity of alcohol as a coping mechanism. But the relationship between sexual violence, substance use, and addiction is much deeper and more complex than that issue alone. One study of patients in an inpatient alcohol and other drug detox unit found that 72 percent of them reported a history of physical or sexual violence. In most cases, that violence started when they were children.[10] Statistics of sexual violence in the United States tell a grim story:

- One in four girls and one in six boys will experience sexual violence before the age of eighteen.
- More than one-third of women who were raped as minors also were raped as adults.
- Twenty-eight percent of male rape victims were first raped when they were ten years old or younger.
- Almost half of multiracial women and 45 percent of American Indian or Alaskan Native women have experienced sexual violence in their lifetimes.[11]
- Surveys find that many LGBTQ populations experience much higher rates of sexual violence than heterosexual and cisgender populations, with the highest rates among bisexual women and transgender people.[12]

An analysis of death certificate data by the National Institute on Alcohol Abuse and Alcoholism found that the number of alcohol-related deaths more than doubled from 1999 to 2017.[13] We have to start making the obvious connections here between sexual violence and addiction.

At the same time as we are seeing women dying in increasing numbers from alcohol consumption, we are being exposed to stories of sexual violence like never before. Since the #MeToo movement went viral in 2017, we have been seeing regular headlines about brave survivors coming forward to speak against their perpetrators. This movement is purposeful, it's empowering, it's vital, and it's necessary to advance the rights and societal treatment of survivors of sexual violence. However, though speaking our truth publicly can be very healing for many of us, we must also acknowledge that the survivors coming forward are being exposed to hate and misunderstanding like never before. We must appreciate the amount of trauma being flung upon everyone when these stories break. From the media intruding into every aspect of a victim's life to the vast number of both uninformed and downright cruel people on social media who insist on shaming, blaming, and even committing more violence on people who speak out about the violence already done to them. The courageous survivors telling their stories on the news are exposed to this, as are all other survivors who are hearing it and being forced to confront their own past traumas. The traumatic memories of our assaults, of our experiences with family and friends who doubted or shamed us, of our involvement with the criminal justice system, and more rush to the surface whenever we hear these stories and see the responses. And if we do not have adequate supports in place, we will reach for whatever negative coping mechanisms we have nearby to help us deal with this surge of trauma.

In a broad sense, we as a nation and a society have not created enough healing spaces and resources to support people when they need it most. In a very specific sense, we as victim advocates, rape crisis providers, and treatment facilities have not been given the resources and support needed to rise and meet the increasing demand for therapeutic services. If we cannot offer resources to those who come forward, then asking them to do so is causing more harm than good.

• • •

Trauma has many layers. The ways in which we choose to cope with our trauma can either peel back those layers so they can begin to heal, or they can compound and harden the layers already there, making it even harder to find and develop our true selves.

Imagine a snowball rolling down a snowy hill. As it rolls down, it speeds up and picks up more and more snow. The ball gets larger and faster as it goes, and it gets harder to stop. This is what happens to us when we have a traumatic experience that is left untreated. If we engage in addictive behaviors in an attempt to avoid and conceal that trauma, we are just continuing to roll downhill. We are collecting other hurts, lies, injuries, and traumas that layer over the others until we become this large ball of hurt speeding faster and faster. It is never impossible to stop rolling, to seek help. But the longer we roll, the more likely we are to stop with a crash. That crash looks very different for each of us. If we're lucky, it could mean a mandated stay in a treatment facility that allows us to find recovery. It could also mean an arrest, an overdose, or the loss of people, jobs, respect, homes. Or it could mean death.

So how do we begin to peel back those layers of trauma? How do we slow down the rolling, stop compounding our pain, and start to heal? The answer may be different for everyone. For me, in the very beginning, it started with addiction treatment. I went to a thirty-day inpatient drug and alcohol rehabilitation program, and it saved my life. This addiction treatment was vital for me because it taught me how to live without the drugs and alcohol that were killing me. It finally proved to me that I had to find alternative ways to cope, and I began to understand that the secrets I was keeping about my traumatic experiences were keeping me sick. After ten years of trauma and addiction, I had to begin peeling back the layers. After treatment, I went on to a halfway house so I could continue learning how to live without my primary unhealthy coping mechanisms. Then I found a safe and supportive therapist and began to truly appreciate how my trauma from being raped had influenced every single aspect of who I was. Once I was able to understand that my responses to the violence I endured were normal and common, I finally started to believe that I could find other ways to cope.

There's one realization I repeat every chance I get: *my self-awareness is my greatest tool in recovery.* In order to begin seeing the *whys* of my feelings and behavior and how I could live differently, I first had to understand myself. Earlier, we talked about how the brain responds to trauma. When we conceal that trauma with drugs and alcohol, we don't give our brain any time or space to heal. Instead of healing, our addictions lead us to compound the stress and damage to our brains and bodies. When we're stuck in a cycle of victimization and unhealthy behaviors, we cannot *think* clearly. So how can we expect to make good choices for ourselves? The first step for many of us is putting down the drinks and drugs so we have a chance to really think. It also gives our bodies a chance to start healing from any physical ailments our addictions have caused. Addiction treatment, sobriety, and Twelve Step or other support meetings are all often part of the solution. But after everything we have been through, stopping our unhealthy behaviors is not enough.

Once we can think clearly, we need to put in the work to really heal our minds. This is hard stuff, and it can be dangerous to try to do it alone. I recommend that you start the process of unpacking your trauma in a therapeutic setting with a trauma-informed counselor. Thankfully, finding a good licensed therapist is not as hard as it used to be. Start with your local resources. Call your local rape crisis center or victim services program and ask if it has a licensed trauma therapist on staff or if it has a list of recommendations. The website for the American Psychological Association (https://locator.apa.org/) has a search tool to help you find a psychologist near you—it also allows you to specify the type of provider you are seeking, such as someone with a specialty in treating addiction or trauma. The website for your insurance company may also have a search tool to help you find a provider in your coverage network. If you do not have insurance, some states have programs that cover expenses for specific counseling services under their crime victim compensation programs. Look up your state's program to find out if you qualify for benefits. Some of the organizations listed at the back of this book may also be helpful in your search.

When you are looking for a therapist, you can ask whether they are trained in practices such as eye movement desensitization and reprocessing (EMDR), cognitive-behavioral therapy, or cognitive processing therapy, which are just some of the therapies that have shown positive outcomes with sexual assault survivors. The key is finding a therapist who is experienced in treating the symptoms you are experiencing and with whom you connect and trust enough to really open up. You may have to try multiple professionals before you find someone who really makes you feel comfortable. The cost of therapy can also be a barrier, even for people who have insurance. And I'm not going to lie to you: once you get into therapy, the work is *hard*. But if you try, and really engage, it is worth it. The time, money, energy, and hard work will lead to a freedom that you have never known. It will mean a release from the grasp of the trauma, helping your brain and body heal, and giving yourself the ability to breathe again. You deserve that. You have been through enough already.

I am not saying that everything will change, but a lot will. If you do the work to find a therapist you really connect with and actively work with them and on yourself, you will be able to live a life free from the tight grasp of trauma and free from the reasons to engage in addictive behaviors. If you take the time to truly understand your own responses to the trauma you have endured and engage in a program or treatment that helps you reprocess that experience, you will get one of the key elements to living life on your own terms: self-awareness.

"Okay," you may be thinking, "but what can I do to help quiet my trauma and deal with triggers *right now*?" Again, that's a great thing for you to discuss and process with your therapist, as everyone is different. But I'll tell you about some tools that help me. Which tool I turn to depends on how I'm feeling in the moment. If I am feeling emotionally overwhelmed and cannot breathe, then first things first: I must breathe. I need to take at least ten long, deep breaths with my eyes closed. If my primary feeling is stress or anxiety, or I need help focusing on a task, I'll grab my headphones and turn on some calming music. I recommend trying the app Insight Timer. It uses a particular kind of music called *bilateral beats,* which incorporates certain tones that play in one ear and then in the other ear, helping to stimulate the brain in a way that eases anxiety. In fact, I am listening to this music as I write this book. That's a good reminder that even after the twenty-some years I've been doing this work, living with trauma is *still hard.* Thinking and writing about my experiences still brings up anxiety and uncomfortable feelings. So no matter where you are on your healing journey, no matter how long you've been dealing with this, know you are not alone in what you are feeling.

Another feeling that my trauma commonly triggers is anger. No matter how much therapeutic work I have done, the anger still comes up at times. Sometimes it feels like a tsunami of hate, fear, love, and confusion. And if I am not spiritually or emotionally prepared for this surge, it has the potential to destroy a lot of good things in my life. Let me be clear here: anger is normal. As a survivor and person in recovery from addiction, I consider anger a huge part of my journey. It is common for those of us who have been harmed, oppressed, and discriminated against to have anger. Anger is not always negative. If we think about the shit that we have been through, have repressed, and have been forced to be silent about, we are rightfully pissed off. The widespread cover-ups of sexual violence, the silencing of survivors, and the inequalities present in our country's government and justice system are enough to anger anyone. Add sexual trauma into the mix, and it's a wonder we ever manage to *not* feel angry. This anger is justified. It's more than okay—for many of us, it is a requirement to tap into that anger and walk through it if we ever want to heal.

The harmful side of the anger comes when I can tell it's causing me more stress than it's worth. Or when it spills out onto people I love—people who are trying to love and help me and don't deserve to be the targets of my anger. The value, or lack thereof, in my anger lies in how I process it. When I recognize that anger is the primary emotion I'm experiencing, I need a physical release. Sometimes that means switching my calming music to some hard-core metal or rock and scream-singing at the top of my lungs. Usually, I need to couple the music and screaming with some other physical activity. So I will either clean the house (which, let's face it, helps everyone!), or I will physically exhaust my body by running, lifting weights, or jumping on my exercise bike and riding as fast as I can.

I will never forget one morning when I woke up in a particularly foul-ass mood. I'm always the first one up in my house. My wife loves to sleep in, and though my little guy usually gets up around 6:30 or 7 a.m., he loves to slip into our room to cuddle in our bed. Both he and my wife will spend as much time in bed as they can. Not me. The minute my eyes open, I'm already thinking about what I need to do—emails to send or return, writing to work on. I love to harness the early morning hours.

On this morning, I was up and on my exercise bike by 6 a.m. My bike has a screen with both live and on-demand classes you can stream. I selected an extra-intense kick-ass ride with music that always gets me going. I wear headphones, but quite frankly, they're useless. Because once I get into it, I usually start singing. On this particular day, the song "What About Us" by P!nk came on, and my scream-singing began. I didn't even realize how loudly I was singing until the class ended and I checked my phone. I saw a text from my wife with a photo of her and my three-year-old son with horrified looks on their faces. The caption read, "What about Us??????" It was followed by another text with a bunch of hearts that said, "We love you so much baby, work it out!" I laughed so hard. It was exactly what I needed to release the final bits of anxiety and stress and anger from my body. I jumped into bed and snuggled them both with gratitude. You cannot put a price tag on that level of unconditional love.

Writing is another amazing tool for me. Whether you write in a journal every day or just pick up a pen or hit the keyboard when your brain is being hijacked by a trigger, getting all your thoughts (negative, positive, or indifferent) out of your head and onto the paper or screen is always a good release. If you're feeling particularly vulnerable or are scared of someone else seeing what you wrote, you don't even have to keep the writing when you're done. Just rip that shit up or burn it or shred it, and throw it all away.

• • •

I think many of us living with trauma tend to downplay the effects we experience on a daily basis. That's understandable—we don't have time to deal with that shit! We have kids, and work, and laundry, and three dogs to walk, and a partner or family member who requires more of our attention. All of these can be excellent excuses to avoid our own stuff. But just reading this book is a huge step toward focusing on yourself and the effects of your trauma. Hopefully, you're starting to better understand yourself and recognize the ways trauma manifests in your life. Maybe you're even starting to develop a plan for how to heal. Regardless, you already deserve major kudos!

For me, recovery can feel like both a blessing and a curse, because, to paraphrase Maya Angelou, now that I know better, I must do better. I can no longer cling to denial or fall back on ignorant bliss. I have been taught the skills and given the tools I need to deal with my trauma, so I no longer have an excuse not to use them. But every day, I'm still learning. I'm always having new epiphanies about myself and figuring out ways to deal a little better. I hope your main takeaway from this chapter is the need to learn more about yourself and how trauma has manifested in your life. Even more important, I hope you're starting to believe that it is possible to cope and heal in a healthy way—without drugs and alcohol and other behaviors that do more harm than good. It will take work, and it won't happen overnight, but you can do it. You don't have to let what happened to you control your life anymore.

EXERCISE

Now that we have learned how trauma impacts us and some of the common effects for survivors, start examining the effects of trauma in your life. Think about how you usually respond when trauma-related emotions come up. In your notebook, write about the following:

- If something makes you mad, what is your usual first response? Do you think this response is helpful or unhelpful? What are other helpful ways you can deal with anger?

- When you notice you are sad, what is your usual response? Do you think this response is helpful or unhelpful? What are other helpful ways you can deal with sadness?
- When you notice you are anxious or stressed, what is your usual response? Do you think this response is helpful or unhelpful? What are other helpful ways you can deal with anxiety?

Next time you experience these emotions, try some of the new responses you came up with. You will not do this perfectly for, like, the first hundred times, so please be gentle with yourself. Keep working on it, ask a therapist for other ideas, and you will start noticing a difference. Even if you can interrupt a typical unhealthy response for just a second and become aware of it enough to think about the change you want, that is progress. Celebrate that.

Meditation

Today, I will honor myself by allowing myself the freedom to be human. The reasons for my coping behaviors are larger than myself, and they will take time to change. Nothing truly worth having in life comes freely. The best gifts I can give myself today are being aware of my feelings and taking care of myself. With time, I have the power to change.

Mantra

I deserve to be free from the effects of my trauma. I will not beat myself up for my coping behaviors. I have been through enough already.

3

Honesty

*I began tuning in to the gut feelings that I had buried for so
many years—that inner moral compass that told me when
something wasn't in my best interest. But, I still hadn't quite
mastered how to actually change my behaviors.*

—BLACKOUT GIRL, PAGES 218–219

ONE OF THE CORNERSTONES OF A SOLID RECOVERY is the
ability to be fully honest in all of our endeavors. This is hard
for those struggling with trauma and addiction, especially in the
beginning. In the past, we have spent lots of time and energy calculating how to cover up and hide our addictions, wounds, and
secrets. That is a really hard habit to break, especially considering why we do it in the first place. Dishonesty is a tool we've used
for self-preservation. It is very common for survivors to believe
that how we have responded to sexual violence and what we have
done to cope with our trauma is bad and wrong, and we are bad
and wrong people because if it. We'll examine this internalized
shame and how to deal with it in the next chapter. For now, it's
important to recognize that lying, omitting the truth, and all
kinds of dishonesty have helped us cover up and deal with our
feelings when we couldn't see any other solution. Sometimes we
lie to protect others; sometimes we lie to protect ourselves. It's

often easier to avoid the pain of the *why* we seek to use and conceal. For many of us, the lies we tell ourselves and the lies we tell others have shaped our very existence.

When the lies fall away, who am I? What is left? What part of the story I tell myself or others is fact versus fiction? Can I even tell the difference anymore? These are often the questions that plague us in early recovery. They keep us up at night. What if the world discovers we are not who we have portrayed ourselves to be all these years? What if we don't even know who we are? The lies we tell have built a fortress around us and, in many cases, inside of us. We cannot distinguish our truth from the lies we have told, and we are petrified that as we recover, we will be exposed in more ways than we can handle.

The beauty of working any recovery program is this: it is a new start. We get a fresh page. A clean slate. Everything that happened prior to this point, everything we did and said, can be shifted and put into a new context. That's not to say that our past behaviors don't matter—all of our actions, thoughts, and deeds must be held into account in a meaningful way. But they can fade into our history as we make an active choice to be a different person. A choice to gain that vital self-awareness and make healthy choices. This work must begin on the inside first.

Making amends is Step Nine in Twelve Step recovery programs. I have seen many people come into addiction recovery for the first time and try to tackle all their amends right away. Some people think that if they do everything possible to immediately make right every bad thing they've done, they will be free and exonerated from their actions. Making amends to others we have hurt is vital recovery work, but there is a reason it comes far later in our addiction recovery program and needs to come later in our trauma-healing journey as well. First and foremost, you must contend with yourself. You need to distinguish who you are now from who you were then. You have to fully understand your own thoughts, feelings, and actions before you can atone for them. Otherwise, your amends for bad deeds will ring as hollow as when a child tells the truth just to gain a reward. When a child hits a friend on the playground, their parents will usually make them apologize, right? They apologize but then do the same thing again a day later. This is because the child is learning. Their brain is still developing. They do not yet fully comprehend what is right or wrong. They act on pure instinct based on their own needs. This is normal development.

In early addiction recovery, we are like toddlers in many ways. We're either learning many things for the first time or relearning them because our use of drugs and alcohol has stunted our growth and development. We may have to learn how to hold down a job, how to cook healthy food, how to pay our bills on time. We also have to learn who we are, where we belong, and how we want to behave in our new, improved life. When we stop feeling, stop processing, and stop actively participating in life by anesthetizing ourselves, we lose so much. We lose time, we lose experience, we lose the ability to respond appropriately to things happening around us. We lose boundaries, and we lose ourselves. *Truth* and *lie* become so enmeshed that we have trouble telling them apart. We determined that it's much easier to catch a new high or lose time in a bottle than to actually deal with our shit. In early recovery, we can't handle that lifestyle anymore. We must now give ourselves the room to learn how to live in a healthy way.

We have to fully understand the *why* behind our actions before we can really give and gain forgiveness. On a practical level, amends made too soon and without this framework are often not received well. It is obvious to the person being "apologized" to that this is simply an act, rather than a true understanding of or appreciation for the harm done. It can do more harm than good. Have you ever been on the receiving end of an apology when it was clear it was given only for the reward, not because the person apologizing truly understood the harm done? It's infuriating. In recovery, we have to be vigilant of our intentions. We have to understand that our dishonesty has led to harm, and that harm will take time to repair. Like any true repair, this must start from within. If you hear someone refer to early recovery being a very selfish program, this is what they mean. You have to focus on and unravel yourself. You have to begin to unpack your lies, your actions, your reasons, your faults, and your motives to begin to understand yourself. And you have to focus on yourself before you can focus on anyone else.

Twelve Step programs of recovery require this work be done through a *personal inventory*—an extensive list or narrative of past behaviors, acts, or thoughts that you now believe were harmful. An inventory is helpful and can lead to great discoveries and important realizations. However, asking someone to suddenly disclose an entire life's worth of pain, secrets, and fears can also be very unrealistic and potentially harmful. As survivors of sexual violence, we must have appropriate space and time to unpack our pain. Trying to do this work all at once, and in a forced or prescriptive way, could lead us directly into relapse.

As a disclaimer, I want to say this: there are many pathways to healing and recovery, and while my experience comes from the use of some Twelve Step programs, I also realize that they had vital flaws and were not helpful, safe, or supportive at all times. I had to seek other resources to fully recover and heal. You may need to do the same. You may never wish to walk into a traditional Twelve Step meeting, and that is okay. As long as you can find a supportive mechanism that works for you, do that. If you want to cobble together your own program of recovery, that works too. That is basically what I did. I did not find it all in one place, and as I have evolved in recovery, I rarely go to meetings anymore. I find my peace in other places. With that said, I did gain a strong foundation using methods that traditional Twelve Step programs offered me, and I used the meetings to find accountability, strength, mentors, and community. This allowed me to stabilize and grow. So whether or not you work a Twelve Step program yourself, maybe the insights I have gained from this work can be useful for you too.

• • •

Traditional Twelve Step recovery meetings are not safe spaces for survivors to speak up about their experiences with sexual violence. Many in Twelve Step programs would call that an *outside issue,* meaning an issue outside of the meeting's focus on substance use, and potentially shut a survivor down by cutting them off or dismissing their pain.

This is why many survivors need different peer support services to either replace or complement Twelve Step programs. Discovery and disclosure of past sexual violence need time and space to happen. Most survivors have spent many years, maybe even their whole lives, running from or trying to conceal their past. I used to think my secrets would kill me if I ever let them out. It took me a long time in recovery to truly internalize that the exact opposite was true. When I allowed my secrets to remain locked inside, they held so much power over me. They owned me. If we're asked to just dump all of our secrets out at once, it can be overwhelming.

We also have to consider how trauma impacts the brain and memory. Remember what we learned in the first chapter. Survivors of traumatic experiences very rarely remember details in a linear fashion. They often cannot sit down and simply write down what happened and when. This reality makes a full and complete inventory a bit challenging for some. Everyone experiences trauma differently, and everyone heals and releases their experiences differently. Some people can remember their traumatic experiences very clearly; others cannot. This is why it's important to listen to yourself, be gentle, and ask for guidance from a professional. We each need to learn what process works best for us, and, for many of us, the Twelve Step inventory process alone is not going to work well.

When I first got clean and sober, I had to ease into honesty, both with myself and others. I had to learn, first and foremost, that I no longer had anything to hide in my daily life. This was incredibly liberating. When I woke up each morning, I knew I had a clean slate. Before I went to bed at night, I did an inventory of my day. Did I hurt anyone today? Did I behave in a way that could have led to my own or someone else's pain and suffering? If so, I would either write about that experience or talk it through with a friend or a sponsor in my recovery circle. This can be very difficult to do. Even to this day, writing or speaking about my past mistakes can bring up a lot of feelings. When writing gets too intense, I get up and walk away. I do something else for a while—maybe exercise, organize some part of my home, cry, scream. But I always come back to it.

Sometimes I may need only a few minutes to write out what I'm thinking. Other times I need hours, and in some cases, days or weeks. When I'm digging deep into an issue that really hits home with me or I'm detailing a painful experience, it can feel like the keyboard is on fire. My hands retreat from it like hot coils. Sometimes this means I'm right where I need to be, and I push through and into the emotions. Other times, this feeling means that I need to stop and give myself room to feel what is rising inside. It's okay to give yourself time to explore what comes up as you start doing this work. This is necessary. The important thing is to be honest with yourself and not just avoid the task.

This work is hard, and it is painful. Believe me, I can't blame anyone for wanting to avoid it. Unfortunately, we survivors in recovery have to experience uncomfortable emotions. Avoidance is simply continuing our pattern of running away from the things we need to confront. It may be hard for you to decipher whether stepping away from this work is actually helpful or just a reason to avoid it. It may be so ingrained in you to shut down emotionally that, when presented with the fear, shame, and anger of your past and present, you shut down automatically. Part of the work is figuring out your patterns and what is best for you, both in the moment and in your long-term recovery.

When we first start identifying our pain in an honest way, we may be flooded with emotions. We need to hold sacred space for those emotions. We need to understand the power they have in our lives and in our overall wellness. We also need to appreciate the purpose of them. These feelings have often acted as triggers in our active addictions, so we must take special care to ensure we are in a safe space to evaluate them properly. We must dissect them and hold them up in front of us. We must try to understand them and where they came from. Then, we can slowly start to dismantle and disempower them. This requires brutal honesty. This requires stepping into the flame, not away from it. In these moments, I want you to know this: *you are okay.* These feelings, while intense and consuming, can be reprocessed for healing and empowerment. This is the core of the hard work. To sit with a feeling long enough to let it pass is to know great strength and mastery of our emotions.

You may not be able to do this alone at first, and that is okay. If trying to do this alone is so uncomfortable that you immediately reach for an old habit that could hurt you, please stop. Consider doing this in the presence of a therapist, a sexual violence survivor support group, a Twelve Step sponsor, or another healthy, loving person. A sponsor is a person in a Twelve Step program who is there to help you navigate recovery. They are someone who has been clean and sober for at least a year, and they should be someone you trust and can access readily. If you are not engaging in a Twelve Step program, or your sponsor doesn't have experience with sexual trauma recovery, ask a therapist or trusted friend to be with you while you do this work. If you are not at a place where you trust anyone with your stuff yet (which is also okay), then writing it down and owning it yourself is the best place to start. Just continue being gentle with yourself, stepping away when you need to, and returning to the task when you can.

No one can take away the pain you are feeling or will feel in these moments. I cannot promise that it won't hurt again. Our past will always be a part of us, and it will likely come up from time to time and hurt to some degree. What I can promise you is this: if you are fully honest with yourself, if you allow yourself to experience what is coming up for you in a brutally honest way, if you give yourself the care and space to feel the feelings rising inside of you—you will make it to the other side, and it will get better. Depending on the intensity of the situation or the emotion you are feeling, it may get worse before it gets better. Actually, that's a good sign. That means you are actually feeling it, experiencing it in its most honest and raw form. But slowly, over time, it will lessen. It will lose its power over you.

This is such hard work because it is an attempt to completely reverse our old ways of thinking. We ran, drank, used, self-harmed, and did more to escape our feelings. And now I'm saying we must welcome these feelings, embrace them. It will feel wrong at first, but this is one of the major keys to our freedom. The ability to be honest—to make a mistake, own it, and forgive ourselves for it—is an amazing gift that recovery will give us. But only if we are truly open and willing. Being honest with ourselves is hard work, but it is a vital, lifesaving investment in our futures. Nothing worth having in life is gained without struggle. You are worth the struggle.

If you go to a Twelve Step meeting, you'll hear this honesty practice referred to as "keeping our side of the street clean." When I was using, my side of the street looked like trash day in New York City. It was messy, and it smelled like shit. Even after I was sober, I would often still find myself telling little stupid lies. I would notice them as they came out of my mouth, and I would be like, *Wait, why the hell did I just do that?* I would be so embarrassed and ashamed, and I would talk about it with my sponsor. She would gently remind me that *I was learning.* Changing our behavior is *hard.* It is not something that happens overnight. When I caught myself returning to an unhealthy behavior, I would share about it in a meeting or with my therapist and work through it. I would be honest about it, and that enabled me to see it for what it was: a learned behavior. And it didn't form in a vacuum. I learned to lie because I spent my young life not feeling free to speak up, not feeling safe to share and to be honest.

For those of us who are survivors of sexual trauma, this realization is a huge piece of our puzzle. If our abuse occurred in secrecy, like so much sexual violence does, there is that added layer of never feeling safe or free to speak about what we experienced. Being honest about it may have never seemed possible for a variety of reasons. Maybe we did try to speak about it and were punished or further silenced in other ways. I will never forget working with an amazing group of survivors who had all been sexually abused at the hands of Catholic priests. I met many of them during the release of a Philadelphia grand jury report in 2005, and then when another one was released in 2011, many survivors and victims began to reach out to me. These brave men and women changed my life, and I am forever indebted to their stories, their pain, and their bravery. Many of them were abused as very young children. When the abuse was discovered by an adult, whether a parent or someone else, the Catholic Church used the full force of its power to silence the victims and their families, both legally and emotionally. Church leaders abused their power as spiritual counselors to make victims feel responsible or unworthy of God's love and to drive them further into their own guilt and shame. These leaders also tangled victims up legally with binding agreements that explicitly stated that if they talked to anyone about the abuse they endured, they would face dire legal or financial consequences.

These contracts are called nondisclosure agreements (NDAs) and, up until a few years ago, they were commonplace both in the Catholic Church and in most corporations. You may be familiar with NDAs from the Harvey Weinstein case. Weinstein used cash payouts and a signature in an attempt to silence his victims. Yet many survivors of abuse by Weinstein and other high-profile perpetrators who signed NDAs have decided to speak up, in spite of the potential consequences. This has sparked a public condemnation of forcing victims of sexual harassment and violence to sign NDAs, and many organizations have pledged to stop using them in these cases. After many grand jury reports and discoveries of evidence in the Catholic clergy sexual abuse cases, the Catholic Church finally relented and stated that it would never legally hold a victim to an agreement they had signed in the past. This removed chains of silence from thousands of survivors and gave them their truth back. After public scrutiny and pressure over Matt Lauer's use of these documents to silence women while he was an anchor on NBC's *Today* show, the network also released a similar statement. If you have signed an NDA or other legal document that keeps you from speaking about the crimes perpetrated against you, I recommend speaking with an attorney with experience in this area.

• • •

If we want to experience real joy, we must first experience pure honesty. We must be able to list our experiences and unpack what they meant to us and how we hold them in our bodies, minds, and spirits. We must be able to pull them out from the dark corners of our minds and hold them to the light. Then, when we are ready, we can decide to share them with other people.

The truth will set you free. I know that's a cliché, but it is so true for us. We cannot achieve emotional freedom without the truth. Some survivors have repressed their memories and have never truly realized all the ways in which they were abused. But when the clouds of drugs and alcohol begin to clear, the memories often surface. This is why it's so important to have a plan for how to examine these memories in a safe way as they come up. And why, if possible, you should find a professional you trust to help you. As we have learned, our feelings cannot destroy us, but our avoidance of them can hurt us. So while you may never have spoken your truth for a variety of reasons, know that you can. That truth is *yours*, and no one else owns it. The first step is the simple, gentle acknowledgment that it's okay to tell the truth. That alone is a huge victory. Releasing our secrets will set us free. In his book *The Body Keeps the Score*, psychiatrist Bessel van der Kolk explains this in a very poignant way: "As long as you keep secrets and suppress information, you are fundamentally at war with yourself. . . . The critical issue is allowing yourself to know what you know. That takes an enormous amount of courage."

I have heard survivors say this process feels like dropping the chains that have bound them to their pain. Release yourself. You deserve to be free from the pain.

EXERCISE 1

Think of one experience you have had in your past that haunts you. Write down whatever comes to mind. Don't worry if it doesn't make sense. Don't worry about whether your memory is linear or sounds coherent. Just be honest and write what comes up for you in this moment.

EXERCISE 2

Start making a list of any and all secrets that you are holding on to. What are the things that you quickly try to silence as soon as they rise in your mind? What are the thoughts, actions, behaviors, or feelings that keep you awake at night? No matter how little or big they are, just write them down. If you are struggling to find the words or are too uncomfortable writing them down, start with a more abstract exercise. Draw a suitcase or a house with rooms. In the suitcase or house, draw symbols that represent the secrets you are keeping.

Then, start examining each secret you wrote down. Think about it and try to really understand the role this secret has played in your life. How does this secret make you feel? In what ways did this secret help you? Did this secret cause you pain? If so, how? Did this secret create a snowball of lies in your life? What would that secret do to you if you released it? What response do you think you would have? Who would be your support? What would it look like for you to start releasing the trauma of this secret today? Write down the people, places, or things that could help you bring that secret to the surface.

If you write all this down and then get anxiety about its presence in the world—destroy it. Burn the pages, rip up the writing, shred it, or delete the document. If you want to keep it but worry about someone else finding your writing, put your notebook in a locked drawer, or password-protect your documents. This is real, hard stuff. I want you to be as safe as possible while exploring these feelings.

This is a long-term exercise. Start with whatever comes to mind for you right now and stop whenever you feel the need. Then return to this whenever a new secret comes to you asking for release. Keep your notebook and a pen handy at all times, or use the notes section in your phone. If writing doesn't work for you, keep the phone number of a trusted friend, sponsor, or therapist close by. The key here is that when things come up, we should try to address them as soon as we can. There may be times when something really big rises, and you may need more help to process it. That is when a therapist is super helpful. Bring your notebook to your therapy appointment.

Meditation

I will not run from my past today. I am finding the inner strength to face my demons, my secrets, and my fears. This is a marathon, not a sprint, and I do not need to tackle everything today. One day at a time, I will sort through the wreckage of my past and emerge stronger, free, and peaceful.

Mantra

My secrets no longer own me. If I am gentle with myself, I will move through them and find freedom on the other side.

Shame

*My body was shaking uncontrollably, and I had never felt so
utterly, completely, uncontrollably ashamed.*

—BLACKOUT GIRL, PAGE 16

THE HOLIDAYS THIS PAST YEAR WERE AMAZING but also
hectic. We made a spontaneous decision to get a puppy, and our
foster daughter, Tea, had just given birth to a beautiful baby boy,
Riley, officially making us grandparents. Tea, who now lives with
her boyfriend, and the baby came to stay with us for a few days.
While she was here, we had to take my four-year-old son, Victor,
to the emergency room to get his first (of what I am sure will be
many) stitches. In short, things were a bit stressful.

On Tea and Riley's third night with us, I was sitting on the
couch holding the baby while Tea was in the shower. My wife
had taken the puppy out for a walk, so I was also watching Victor. He was both jealous of the baby and very intrigued. Both
Victor's interest in Riley and his energy were in high gear. I
had to keep correcting him: "No, Victor, you cannot jump on
the couch when I am holding the baby." "No, Victor, he is not
ready for your stuffed animal to be shoved in his face." "No,
Victor, I cannot come play with you. I am holding the baby."

Just as I got the baby soothed enough to fall sleep, Victor walked over and opened both the front door and the screen door, sending a burst of cold air through the house. I quietly asked, "Victor, what are you doing? Honey, close the door." He gave me a childlike look that communicated he was too wound up to listen to reasonable instructions. I thought, "Oh boy. Here we go."

I tried a more stern response: "Victor, close the door. Riley is sleeping, and it's freezing out."

"No!" Victor responded, full of defiance.

My voice elevated. "Victor, close the door!"

"NO!"

He screamed and proceeded to walk to the back door and also open that door wide open. Then he stormed back to me as cold air began to fill the house and once again screamed, "NO!"

I lost my shit.

Exactly what happened is a little blurry. From what I recall, I stood up, still holding the sleeping baby, and proceeded to scream my head off at my son. Of course, Victor began to cry.

As soon as Victor started crying, the baby did as well. Then I realized what a maniac I had become. My rational mind kicked in, and I knew that yelling at a child does nothing but give you a hoarse voice and a boatload of guilt and shame. It does nothing to change the behavior or teach the child anything.

I closed both doors and told Victor to go to his room. Tea was done with her shower, so I gave the baby to her and went into my own room to calm down a bit. I was filled with shame.

How could I have done that? What is wrong with me? I am a horrible mother. I am a horrible person. Why would I yell at that little person I love so dearly?

Eventually, my wife came into the room. She knew something was seriously wrong, so she proceeded carefully. I looked up, tears streaming down my face, and I started unloading all the horrible things I was saying to myself. She held me for a while until I was coherent enough to explain what happened. By then, I knew what I had to do next. I needed to apologize to my son. I went into his room and saw that he had already stopped crying and was playing with some toys. He sheepishly looked up at me. He knew he had misbehaved. I began a gentle conversation about why he opened the doors, why Mommy asked him to close them, and why I got so upset when he refused to listen. Then, I apologized for yelling. I explained to him that I lost my temper, I was not proud of it, and I was sorry. I told him that I should have responded differently, and we then discussed his part of the ordeal. It was not okay to open doors when it was freezing and dark out, and it was not okay to choose not to listen to Mommy. He then offered an apology as well.

I got into bed that night covered in shame. I was glad I had made amends with Victor, but I hated how I responded. I hated that I got so frustrated and felt so powerless that I felt the need to yell at him. I began googling "yelling at children." This did not help my emotional state. Don't do that.

Then my wife and I had a really good conversation. We went through all of the things I could have done differently, how I could have engaged his defiance differently without losing my shit and thus losing any hope of a teachable moment for me or Victor. I then had to grapple with the very real fact that I am human. I make mistakes. *And that is okay.* I went to bed with a whole lot less shame and more understanding.

This incident is a great example both of how much I have grown in my recovery and of how even those of us who have been working on ourselves for more than twenty years will make mistakes. If something like this had happened twenty years ago, I would have been up all night beating myself up. Back then, I didn't have the tools to process the incident, to make amendments, or to speak openly and humbly with another person about my actions. This is the power of shame. If we let it, it will beat us up and beat us down. If we don't address it and extinguish it at its source, it can control us.

• • •

I recently had an excellent conversation with Dr. Michele Pole, a clinical psychologist who, at the time, was running the women's trauma unit at an addiction treatment center. We started to talk about addiction, victimization, and trauma. As I shared my personal story with her, we turned our attention to the role of shame in addiction and trauma. As we've discussed in previous chapters, many of us have used our addictive substances and behaviors in an attempt to bury thoughts and emotions we don't want to face. Very often, the primary emotion people with addiction and trauma are seeking to conceal is a deep and overwhelming sense of shame.

For survivors of sexual violence, our shame can feel as thick as quicksand—it continuously pulls us down into a deep abyss of self-loathing and despair. During our conversation, Dr. Pole said something that resonated with me very deeply. She said, "Shame is an emotional cancer that, if left untreated, will just eat away at a person."

For so many years in my childhood and into early adulthood, I knew my shame was there—it was like this dark passenger that never left my side. It would fester beneath the surface at all times, keeping me just low enough to feel subhuman. It most loved to emerge when I was experiencing a nice emotion like pride, joy, or excitement. At the worst times, the shame would creep up like a slithering snake and snatch the good right out from under me. Whenever I had a moment of relief, it would return to remind me that I was unworthy, that I was bad, that I was dirty. This is the insidious nature of shame; its sole intent is to destroy us, and it's an inside job. Shame has been the most intense feeling I've experienced as a result of my trauma. Dr. Pole's description of shame as an emotional cancer made perfect sense to me. That is exactly what it feels like—an emotional cancer that, if left untreated, will devour us. If that seems extreme, I can promise you it isn't. Overwhelming shame almost killed me multiple times. Internalized shame, coupled with the shame others put on us by telling us we are to blame for our victimization, leads survivors of sexual violence to deep addiction, self-harm, and suicide far too often. *Merriam-Webster* defines *shame* as "a painful emotion caused by consciousness of guilt, shortcomings, or impropriety." For us, shame is silence we keep, the stories we hide.

• • •

My long, insidious struggle with shame began when I was first raped at age twelve. No matter what anyone said to me, I was convinced that I was to blame. It wasn't until many years later in recovery that I slowly began to unpack my secrets and realize the truth. As I revisited the experience of being raped and all of its ugly aftermath, I began to see that I was not the cause of my pain. My years of trauma and addiction stemmed from another person's actions against me. My rapist was the person who should feel ashamed, not me. This realization gave me a bit of freedom from the shame that was owning me. But I still didn't realize how long this feeling would cling to me. No matter how much I reminded myself that I wasn't the cause of the violence perpetrated against me, shame kept rearing its ugly head for years into my recovery.

One of the most significant moments in my battle against shame occurred in my late twenties, when I first started working as a victim advocate. I had just celebrated six years of sobriety when I took on the case of a twelve-year-old rape victim. When I looked at her, I had the realization that, being in my twenties, I was about the same age as my rapist had been, and I was working with a twelve-year-old survivor. It was jarring. I looked at this incredibly brave but incredibly vulnerable twelve-year-old, and she looked *so young*. Memories rushed back of myself when I was her age: my oversized bright yellow Swatch rugby shirt, my dark Levi's jeans, my sneakers. My face came into focus: my young, childlike face, with a spattering of freckles bridging my nose from ear to ear. I really saw myself for the first time as I was then. A young child.

Until that moment, whenever I had thought of myself on the day of my rape, I seemed older somehow. I didn't think of myself as being that young, vulnerable child. I think this may be because that horrible, life-changing event did make me older in some ways. The feelings and responsibilities that I suddenly had to confront forced my mind and spirit into an adulthood that did not fit, and I began to think of my external self the way my internal self felt. It wasn't until I saw this twelve-year-old girl, in all her innocence and childlike being, that I could see myself as I really was at that age.

Trauma and shame change the way we see ourselves. I had been doing some intense work for a long time to deal with my own shit from being raped, but this realization had never come up for me. This piece of my puzzle did not slip into place until I worked on that case. I never articulated any of this to my client, because it wouldn't have been appropriate or helpful to her in any way. I was there to provide her with emotional support as she went through her trial. But inside, without knowing it, she gave me a huge gift. It was the gift of seeing myself as who I really was at that moment of incredible victimization. A child. A little girl who was not asking for someone twice her age to have sex with her. A child who should have been protected by an adult, not taken advantage of by one. I was a child when I was raped. And that realization hit me hard, hard enough to shatter a thick layer of shame that was still iced inside of me. I had no idea I was still holding on to so much until I began to thaw, and a new sense of forgiveness came over me. I was able to see that little girl as separate from myself in a way that was so purposeful and important. I was able to hold her in the light of truth and love her and comfort her in a way I had never done before. It was so freeing.

Shame attacks us in our emotional center. It attacks our self-esteem and tells us lies about ourselves. It also overwhelms our ability to counter these lies with logic or self-love. Shame tells us we are bad, we are evil, we are to blame, we are dirty, we are not worthy. Shame is the soundtrack for all of those negative thoughts that play over and over in our heads. When you have experienced sexual assault, shame is often the first emotion to rear its ugly head and take over. When you layer substance use on top of that as a means to cope, it's like splashing lighter fluid onto a bonfire. It may seem to help at first, but we soon find that it only gives the shame more power.

As I did more and more work in recovery, I learned just how universal these feelings are among survivors of sexual violence and addiction. When I spoke with other survivors about my shame, everyone immediately understood. For each one of us, shame created what felt like an impenetrable wall between our past or present abuse and the future lives we want to have. When I tell my story publicly, I look around the room, searching for the shame in the crowd. When I'm done speaking, survivors will always approach me and share their own experiences. Often, I already know who will approach me, because I have spotted that look of shame in their eyes, in the way they sit and carry themselves. It's palpable. Some will say I'm the first person to whom they have ever told their story.

The power of shame as a barrier in our recovery and personal growth is something many people don't understand. *It's just a feeling, right? Can't you just get over it, shake it off?* I cannot tell you how many times I've heard people say things like, "Why can't you just let it go?" to me and other survivors. The misunderstanding is that they think we have control over shame, when in many ways, we do not. In the previous chapter, we talked about the importance of honesty in our recovery. Shame is so crucial to recognize and heal from because it's what keeps us imprisoned in secrecy and silence. It's what keeps us trapped in these lies and prevents us from sharing our truth with others who can help us. When we step back and look at things objectively, maybe for a moment we can recognize that these messages are lies. Of course we're not to blame for our trauma! We are victims of sexual violence—it should be obvious that the person to blame is the person (or people) who victimized us. But given the world we live in, it's also not very surprising that we continue to blame ourselves. Despite the increased and more compassionate media coverage of the past few years, many people still don't fully understand the causes and effects of sexual violence and addiction. We still live in a world where many automatically assume that someone with an addiction is weak or immoral. Similarly, victims of sexual violence are blamed more heavily than our perpetrators. People we used to consider friends, family, or trusted professionals often do anything they can to create distance between us and them. These behaviors and assumptions add layers of societal shame to our arsenal of emotional baggage.

I once attended a conference where Carl M. Dawson, a licensed counselor who specializes in the treatment of substance use disorder and post-traumatic stress disorder (PTSD), discussed how our brains respond to stress, trauma, and substance use. Much of it was information I already knew, some of which I shared in the first chapter of this book, so I listened and nodded along. Then he began to discuss shame and its impact on the brain. He showed some images of brain scans that illustrate what trauma does to the brain. He showed images of brains that have never experienced trauma next to brains that had experienced trauma, and you could see areas of the traumatized brain lit up, showing the impact of the trauma. This made sense to me. Those of us who have had significant traumatic experiences, such as sexual violence, show heightened activity in the sensory part of our brains, where our traumatic memory is stored. Then he came to a slide that completely changed the way I think about shame. He said, "Shame is not truly an emotional experience; it is a biological response to trauma." I froze in my chair. Wait, what?

He went on to show the brain scans of a person hit by a bus. Obviously, being hit by a bus is a pretty traumatic event, right? Not only because of the physical injuries but also the emotional recovery needed. Then he began talking about how victims experience shame from sexual violence, and he put up a second brain scan showing this effect. The brain of a person hit by a bus and the brain of a person who was sexually assaulted. The two were side by side, and the images from the PET scans showed the brains lit up in the exact same area: the sensory area within the right side of the brain, the emotional center of the brain. He discussed how both of these patients were experiencing an intense shame response and that these images show that shame is not an emotional response to trauma; it is a biological response to trauma. To put it mildly, I was dumbfounded. All of a sudden, I was flooded with understanding. Shame is not something we can just control. It's not that easy. It's not an emotion that can just be shaken off. Trauma changed our brains, and now shame is embedded there.

This knowledge was incredibly empowering for me. It was almost like it gave me permission to be ashamed, which in and of itself is indicative of the power of shame. I knew that shame was one of the primary emotions that I had to tackle in therapy in order for me to heal. I knew that shame was the key to the secrets I kept in my life, which kept me sick. What I never realized was that it was a biological response to my assault. I was more than eighteen years into my recovery, and I still struggled with shame. I was just now learning this crucial piece of information that clearly demonstrated why that was. Seeing my shame as a biological response and not an emotional failing on my part made me feel even more able to dominate it.

This is what understanding and knowledge do for us. This is the heart of empowerment. I have had these powerful *aha* moments throughout my recovery. Those moments when something inside you clicks, and you gain a new level of awareness. It changes you. It shifts your thinking and, therefore, your whole being. That incredible twelve-year-old survivor gave me one of those moments, and Carl Dawson gave me another. My assaults were not my fault, and my shame will never be totally eliminated because it is a biological effect of my trauma. The fact that I was raped will always be true in my life. Just like the fact that I am a person who cannot drink or use substances in a nonaddictive way. Similarly, the fact that I will always have some shame embedded in my brain is just a fact. None of these facts diminish me. They are just facts about who I am as a person, similar to my height or my eye color. They define me in description but not in value. I own them as mine, but they do not own me anymore.

...

If you've done any research or have read about shame before, you have probably heard of Brené Brown. If you haven't, she's a world-renowned author, TED Talk personality, and shame researcher who has coined a theory called *shame resilience*. In her many books and talks, Brown dissects the role shame plays in our lives, in our pain, in our healing, and ultimately in our recovery. Brown also acknowledges that shame is something that never goes away—it is an emotion that we all experience all the time, much like joy, anger, sadness, or excitement. Shame is unavoidable. How we deal with it and experience it is another thing altogether. She talks about how we must allow ourselves to be vulnerable enough to identify shame in our lives. We must be able to talk with ourselves and others about the role shame plays in our lives. We must be able to form connections with other people that allow us the space and comfort to identify when shame emerges and how to put it in its rightful place. We also must be able to realize when we are avoiding shame or using what Brown calls *shame screens.*

A shame screen is a defense mechanism we use when we experience shame as a means to avoid something. Our brain involuntarily invokes our fight, flight, or freeze instinct. Sound familiar? This is the same way we respond to threats and trauma triggers. Shame is a huge trauma trigger that we, as survivors and people in recovery, need to fully understand and prepare for. If we haven't adequately prepared for shame triggers, we will activate a shield, a shame screen. Brown also explains that there are three common types of responses to shame, first defined by Linda Hartling, PhD, and colleagues:

- move away—withdraw, hide, stay silent, keep secrets
- move against—try to gain power over the thing that's threatening us, be aggressive, control
- move toward—seek to please, try to belong[14]

None of these are entirely healthy reactions. They may get rid of the shame feeling in the moment, but none of them will help us in the long term, and none of them actually addresses the root of what is causing the shame. In fact, some of these reactions may even make the current situation worse. But recognizing our basic response instincts allows us to realize that we are currently experiencing shame and can choose an alternative, healthier way to respond. When shame shows up in my life today and manages to take control, I call it *shame spiraling*. Yes, as evidenced by my story at the beginning of this chapter, I am still not immune to shame. Shame is powerful, and even after more than two decades into recovery, it still rears its ugly head from time to time. If I am not in a good emotional space when it shows up, it can consume me. This leads to a shame spiral.

As a result of the ways I've been traumatized in my life, anxiety is a real and ever-present experience for me. Usually my anxiety comes up in the form of a shame response. It's the old voices in my head telling me I am bad, I did something wrong, and I am unworthy of success, love, or acceptance. If I let it go unchecked, it spirals out of control. Picture a drill as it penetrates the surface of the ground—it twists deeper and deeper, spiraling and spiraling, making a deep hole. This is how a shame spiral feels to me. It starts with one thought and unravels into all the bad things that shame makes me think about myself, until I'm deep in a hole. Some people would call this an anxiety attack or panic attack. I prefer to describe it as a shame spiral because that's how it feels to me.

Sometimes I can shut these thoughts and feelings down quickly and remove myself from the spiral. Other times, I spin and spin, and it requires all the tools in my recovery toolbox to get through it. A clearly unhelpful but very common response we survivors have to shame spirals is to *shame ourselves for them*. Sound familiar? Our spiral of shame is telling us that we're weak, we're bad, we're blameworthy, and we think just the very fact that we're in this spiral in the first place, when other people seem to be able to get through life without these kinds of reactions, proves those things to be true. Well, guess what? *That's not true.* Today, when I get into that kind of thinking, I remember those brain images Carl Dawson showed us. As terrible as these shame spirals are when I'm in the midst of them, I know that they are just a part of my recovery. They're part of the way my brain has biologically reacted to the traumatic experiences I had as a child. So when I began to spiral after the emotional outburst with my son, I quickly and gently reminded myself that I do not need to internalize that pain anymore. I was able to shut the shame valve off quickly and rebound from the situation. And as a bonus, I was able to talk through strategies with my wife and learn something!

• • •

The next day, my wife was having a similar frustrating experience with my son. Victor *did not* want to get dressed. This was far from the first time we've had this problem, so we created a song to help Victor with the process. I came into the room and started singing. The song is to the tune of R.E.M.'s "Stand" and goes like this:

Stand in the place where you are
Now face me
Your feet are going to be in these pants
Your head is there to go in this shirt
Now stand in the place where you are
Now you're dressed

His defiance gave way to pure joy as he sang along with me and I helped him get dressed. Later, my wife just looked at me and said, "See, you're a great mom." Any shame I held from the night before evaporated.

• • •

If you've been through addiction treatment or attended Twelve Step meetings, you've probably heard that acceptance is the first step in our addiction recovery. (Literally, it's the First Step in the Twelve Steps.) If we can't accept that we have a problem, how are we supposed to change it? When we accept something as fact, we take most of the power away from it. We can then step away from it and see it as just another part of our lives. Then, we can begin to learn how we deal with this fact. Shame will be a part of every single one of our lives. Sorry, if you were looking for the magic trick to never feeling shame again, I can't give you that. But we *can* control how we deal with it. How we engage with shame and respond to it will make all the difference in our lives. And believe it or not, shaming ourselves for our shame spirals won't do us any good.

So what is helpful when we're in a shame spiral? Personally, I have several tools. First and foremost is the acknowledgment that what I am experiencing is a shame spiral. When my pulse races and my mind begins to tell me horrible things about myself, I remind myself: *These are not facts. These are feelings. These feelings will pass.* I have to tell myself that I am not losing my mind; I am not what the thoughts are telling me I am. Then I will usually grab my headphones and play calming music. This helps to begin to calm the storm in my brain.

Sometimes, I also need to talk. I need to get all the bad thoughts out of my head and expose them and dissect them. It can be really hard for us to sort out our shameful thoughts on our own, and this is where a therapist, partner, or other trusted person who knows our history becomes really helpful. Usually, I turn to my wife, as she is often next to me in bed when a shame spiral strikes. Other times, I will text or call a friend. Typically, I'm not looking for someone to fix my shame or give me suggestions—sometimes hearing other people's suggestions can just increase my shame and anxiety because I can't always do what they are suggesting in the moment. Usually, I just need to be heard. I need someone who knows and respects me to just listen and acknowledge what I'm experiencing. I know that not everyone may have access to a person they would feel comfortable calling in this situation. Especially if you're just starting your recovery, there may be very few people who know about your trauma at all and even fewer whom you would trust to call when you're feeling this vulnerable. And even if you do have a large network of people to turn to, everyone will occasionally need support at a less-than-ideal time, like in the middle of the night, on a busy holiday, or at another time when no one else is available to you. This is why hotlines and online chat rooms for survivors exist. If you need to talk to someone, don't hesitate to use these resources.

Another tool I use is writing. Sometimes all it takes to release myself from the nasty, secret, shameful thoughts slamming around in my head is to get them out and onto paper. Once I see them written out, they do not own me in the same way they did when they were trapped in my head. Exposing them on paper allows the logical parts of my brain to read them and see them for what they are: just hurtful thoughts that are not based on truth.

What if none of these tools work? At certain times in my life, I have turned to prescribed medication. After my dad died, my anxiety was so high my emotions felt like live wires dancing all around me. Not only was I dealing with grief, but I also had huge burdens I was carrying at work. I was busier than I had ever been, working close to eighty hours a week, and much of that work had me steeped in another survivor's trauma. Dealing with all of this at once impacted me tremendously. I got to the point where there were times I thought I was having a heart attack. So I eventually went to the doctor. After a lot of honesty on my part and many physical exams, including an echocardiogram and stress test, my doctor determined that my heart was physically fine. My symptoms were due to the fact that I was under an inordinate amount of stress that I needed to treat. My doctor recommended a low dose of a nonaddictive antianxiety medication. I was hesitant at first, because medication of any kind scares me a bit. But I realized I had to humble myself to the notion that I could not handle all of this on my own, and that was okay.

We have to remember that we are dealing in biology. Sometimes meditation, music, therapy, exercise, and other nonmedical techniques are able to bring us out of a difficult situation, and sometimes they're not. This was a time when I needed more help. You may have encountered people telling you that there is something wrong with taking prescribed behavioral health medications while you're in addiction recovery, whether those medications are to help with your addiction, your trauma, or something else. If so, I'm here to tell you that those people are wrong. Yes, make sure your doctor knows your addiction history. But if you and your doctor think you need medication in order to emotionally regulate yourself and recover, you use medication. There are plenty of nonaddictive medication options for nearly every condition. If you're holding on to any shame about medications, like I was at one time, it's time to let that shit go. Do what your doctor says and take care of your whole self. When you have an infection, you get antibiotics, right? If you have the flu, you go to the doctor. No one would tell you to "just suck it up" when you have a sinus infection or diabetes, right? Of course not. They would say, "Go to the doctor, take your antibiotics, take your insulin."

We need to start normalizing access to mental health medications and medication-assisted addiction treatment. Mental health disorders are just as real and biological as any other illness, and they need to be treated in the same way. They can also be just as impactful and deadly as other serious illnesses. If you're depressed or dealing with extreme anger, sadness, or emotional upheaval due to an emotional wound, go to a clinical psychologist, psychiatrist, or doctor. If you have a therapist, they may be able to give you recommendations on how to talk to your doctor or how to find a psychiatrist who is knowledgeable about addiction and trauma. We must remove the shame associated with getting help. Sometimes the treatment we need will be staying in a treatment center, going to outpatient treatment, or attending support group meetings. Sometimes it's taking medications. There is no moral failing in needing help. So when my doctor looked at me and said, "Your stress level is out of hand, and it has physically impacted you," I listened and I took the medication as prescribed. It helped me get through a really hard time in my life without turning to the very unhealthy self-medication I used to use to deal with that shit.

Another way shame manifests in my life is in the form of anger. Whenever I notice I am getting super defensive or really angry about something, I try to look deeper and figure out what is at the root of that burning rage. Usually for me, it's shame. Often, there is a feeling of unworthiness, a feeling of being less than, self-loathing, or some other kind of internal pain that sparked my anger. In order to get to the *why* of my anger, I have to dissect it and put it all back together like a puzzle. This is the hard work of recovery—really trying to understand yourself, how trauma impacts you specifically, and your basic emotional responses to different situations. It's not easy, but this process can be lifesaving.

• • •

Shame is a really terrible and powerful emotion. I wish I could tell you that if you do X or wait a specific length of time after a traumatic event, you'll never experience shame again. I can't tell you that, because you will keep experiencing it. We all will. We are going to experience everything that life has to offer, and that includes the amazing successes, the heartbreaking losses, the grueling stresses, and the incredible joys. That is life on life's terms. This is what being alive means. For those of us in recovery, what truly matters is how we respond. How we come to understand the role our trauma and addiction play in our lives determines our ability to move forward in recovery and not backward into more trauma and addiction. Self-awareness is the foundation that holds up our recovery. Shame is gonna show up; we cannot change that. But we can shift how we experience it and decide whether it becomes an experience that tears us down or helps us grow.

If shame is an emotional cancer, then the antidotes are love, kindness, compassion, and acceptance. We must realize that we are not the reason for our shame. Shame is a manifestation of our past traumas and pains. It is our brain's response to the horrible things that happened in our lives. Shame is the gatekeeper of those pains, and the only thing that can tame the shame is the way we approach it and transform it. We can transform shame into love in our lives. We can create compassion and kindness for ourselves when shame attempts to enter and steal our joy. We can learn to respond to shame by replacing it with loving-kindness.

EXERCISE

Think and write about how shame shows up in your life today. What does your usual shame response look like? How does it make you feel? Do you have shame screens? If so, what are they? How can you shift your perspective on shame to avoid a shame spiral? When you find yourself in a shame spiral, what tools can you use to pull yourself out safely?

Meditation

Today, I release the shame I carry for all the things that happened to me. I understand that the shame I have experienced is a biological response to my trauma. I am not the cause of that trauma. When shame comes up for me today, I will greet it with kindness and accept it for what it is: my traumatized self needing attention, love, and compassion.

Mantra

The shame I feel is nothing but a symptom of my trauma. I am not my shame response. I am worthy. I am good. Shame does not own me.

5

Humility and Vulnerability

I was the new girl—just as I had been so many times in my
life when entering new schools and towns—and they wanted
to intimidate me. I held my head high, put on my cocky
"don't fuck with me" face, and sat down. I wasn't going to let
them get to me, even though inside I felt more vulnerable
than I had ever been in my life.

—BLACKOUT GIRL, PAGE 196

I STILL VIVIDLY RECALL THE MOMENT when I walked into
my first group session at the addiction treatment center back in
1997. I was clean and sober yet clueless. It was the first time in
a long time that I had to enter a social setting without my usual
sidekicks (drugs and alcohol), and I felt so utterly vulnerable.
Drugs and alcohol had always been my social lubricants—they
were my crutches, my enablers. They allowed me to face anything without having to actually be myself. All of my interactions
were fake back when I was using—nothing I did or said was ever
really based in much reality. I always played tougher than I was
and never allowed myself to be vulnerable. Why should I? I had
been hurt so many times before, both physically and emotionally.
I wasn't going to drop my defenses for anyone.

Growing up, I learned quickly that vulnerability was a sign of
weakness. We did not "share" things in our house—we avoided

emotions as if they were land mines. Laughter was the primary way to resolve conflicts or neutralize difficult topics in my family, so I learned to laugh at myself. When things would get too serious in our home, we made a joke. When things were too painful to deal with, someone would make fun of someone else to sweep the issue under the rug. When anger came into the room, uncomfortable laughter would surely follow. Laughter was the one tie that bound us all together. We relentlessly picked on each other. We were ruthless at each other's expense—all in the hopes that having a laugh would allow us to avoid dealing with anything uncomfortable. No matter how inappropriate the timing, someone in our house knew exactly when to bust out a joke to break the tension.

We each still have keen situational comedic timing to this day. This skill definitely has its uses. I can find the joke in the worst of experiences and make a room full of otherwise-traumatized people bust out laughing. Laughter is one of the best things for the mind, body, and spirit. It releases vital endorphins that help people feel better, it clenches the abdominals and gives a nice quick workout, and it allows people to let their guard down. Laughter can suck the tension out of a room like a vacuum and put people at ease.

However, laughter isn't always healthy. I used laughter as a means to avoid my issues for half my life. I have used laughter to avoid tears, anger, and pain. It's one of my go-to emotional responses, and sometimes, it can be a straight-up cop-out. When I find myself turning to laughter, I have to check in with myself. I have to make sure I'm not using it to cover up something more serious that I need to actually deal with. Laughter can be a great icebreaker, but if I am not careful, I can easily fall straight through the ice and avoid being really present.

One of the most important things I've learned about laughter is that it is not a replacement for feelings. While laughter can be one part of healing, it cannot help you identify how you really feel about an experience and dissect it in the way that's needed in order to fully heal from it. To do that, we need to be truly vulnerable. In chapter 3, we talked about the importance of being honest with ourselves and those around us. Honestly admitting and examining what happened to us, or what we did to others, is the first step in dealing with our trauma. But if we don't couple that honesty with humility and vulnerability, it's honesty without accountability. It's bullshit. We can all throw honesty around while being completely detached from its real purpose. The real purpose in your truth lies in how you feel about it, how you process it, and how you allow it to live in your world. I know this sounds a bit lofty, so bear with me here.

In my active addiction, when I was up all night doing copious amounts of cocaine, I would occasionally open up about things in my past. I would recount painful events to the people with me and think I was being honest and vulnerable. I would tell them the general gist of how I was raped as a child. I would talk about my parents getting divorced, my suicide attempts, and my childhood best friend dying. I would do all the verbal gymnastics that, in the strictest terms, were telling the truth. But I did it all while completely and totally disconnected from any emotional responses connected to these events. I would form words and sentences that told the stories of my past, but I wasn't being truly honest. And I certainly wasn't being vulnerable. I was like a robot spitting out facts to someone, and then I would pat myself on the back while thinking, "Oh, wow, I talked about it. That's good!" Then I would quickly stop thinking about it and often feel shame the next day about revealing these events.

When I got clean and sober and started therapy, I made a big deal out of those "honest" moments. I would tell my counselor that I did indeed talk about my stuff. She gently pointed out that talking about something and feeling something are two separate things. During my years as a traumatized person in active addiction, I became very skilled at emotionally detaching from the events in my life. This skill was lifesaving in many ways—it allowed me to endure unthinkable things in my childhood and teenage years. But once we get into recovery and start actually trying to deal with our past, that shit no longer serves us. It slowly destroys us. In therapy, I began to understand that my truth meant nothing if it wasn't wrapped in all the feelings that went with it. To deal with and start to move past any of the horrific things that happened to me, I had to allow myself to be emotionally vulnerable. After more than twenty years in recovery, this is still the hardest thing for me to do. I do not like being vulnerable. I do not like opening myself up and being exposed. But I have come to understand that this is a requirement in my recovery, so I must actively practice vulnerability every day.

When faced with someone wanting me to be vulnerable, my first instinct is still to be defensive. I might try to make light of the situation or stonewall the person altogether. I can put up emotional walls like a talented mason. I know how to keep people out of my emotional and physical space. One of my former partners nicknamed me "the DA" (the defense attorney) because she said I was defensive about everything. She was not wrong. Being defensive was a part of how I survived sexual assault, years of poor judgment, emotional abuse at the hands of my mother, losing loved ones, and my own self-inflicted trauma. If I could keep you out of my emotional space, then you could not hurt me.

If we truly want to recover from our past hurts, we need to get to a place where we can be vulnerable enough to expose our authentic emotions. This requires honesty backed up with humility and vulnerability. We always have to take a hard look at what we have gone through, and those of us in a Twelve Step program are encouraged to really look at our role in our past, our side of the street. This requires a lot of humility.

. . .

In order to see a past situation in an honest way, we have to let our guard down; we have to loosen our protective grip on our secrets and allow ourselves to be vulnerable. This is not an easy process. As I worked through my experiences with my sponsor and counselor, I encountered many things in my past that I was not proud of. I had to heal from the victimization that happened through no fault of my own, but I also couldn't ignore the other baggage I was carrying: the baggage of my choices in the aftermath of my trauma and in my active addiction. This is a delicate process for a lot of survivors. I had to be careful to separate out the bags that I was responsible for carrying without burdening myself with unnecessary guilt and shame. This part took a lot of humility and vulnerability because I had to trust other people to help me properly divide this up. If we are going to change ourselves, heal ourselves, and become better people, we must be humble enough to admit who we were in our active addictions. This is where that critical Fourth Step in Twelve Step recovery programs can be both difficult and lifesaving.

The Fourth Step in Alcoholics Anonymous, Narcotics Anonymous, and other Twelve Step programs tells us to make "a searching and fearless moral inventory of ourselves." For those of us who have worked a Twelve Step program for addiction recovery without going through trauma-informed addiction treatment or having a trauma-informed therapist to support us, the Fourth Step may have been shoved in our faces as the one and only true way to examine our past. This is where I think traditional Twelve Step programs get it wrong with those of us who have suffered trauma. Yes, we must remove the wreckage of our past; we must be brutally honest with ourselves, air our secrets in a safe environment, and clean up our side of the street. But, in my eyes, the process of cleaning up our side of things and the process of really examining the areas that firmly belong to another person need to stay very separate for those of us who have experienced sexual violence.

The central problem with the Fourth Step for those of us with sexual trauma is that it can easily be interpreted as asking us to blame ourselves for everything that has happened to us. This is the only place in all of the Twelve Steps where we are instructed to unearth our past, eradicate our secrets, and own our shit. But we are told only to inventory *ourselves*. This phrasing immediately lends itself to placing undue blame onto us as the victims and survivors of sexual violence. What happens when a sponsor or another person in the program tells a survivor they must do a moral inventory of all the wrongs in their past? Well, our victimizations are a large part of our past, so it seems logical for them and us to include those victimizations in our inventory, when in reality they should be part of our perpetrator's. This huge disconnect, which can feel a lot like victim blaming, can lead to feelings of failure, frustration, more trauma, and many people walking right out of the rooms of recovery.

There must be an additional step in Twelve Step programs for those of us who are survivors of sexual violence that acknowledges that we have been harmed on a deep level. Most of us have had the mirror turned on ourselves *plenty* of times. We have blamed ourselves, and we have had blame placed on us by people in the justice system, our family, our friends, and our abusers, and sometimes by complete strangers who think they know our situation better than we do. I want to make it clear that doing a moral inventory of ourselves is powerful and necessary. But it should not be the process we use to look at our past abuse and victimization histories. If we feel the need to examine our role, or lack thereof, in any of the abuse that has happened to us, that should be done with a counselor, trauma specialist, or therapist—not with an untrained person in our Twelve Step program. No matter how wonderful and sensitive our Twelve Step sponsor may be, even if they are a survivor of sexual abuse as well, this work is so delicate that we can only be certain of our safety in the hands of a trained and trusted professional.

There are many ways we can help support ourselves during this process. We can use the tools and exercises in this book. We can process our feelings with a writing or journaling practice. We can find and attend support groups specific to sexual trauma. And we can focus on self-care daily. It is important for us to understand how our traumatic experiences have informed our decisions thereafter. And if we engaged in actions that were destructive to ourselves and others, then those actions are appropriate to discuss with our sponsor in our Fourth Step work. But the sexual violence perpetrated on us should not be placed in the same category. That is something that happened *to us*. It is vital for us to understand the impact of our traumatic experiences and the role *they played* in shaping who we are, but we should never be asked to sit down and look at *our part* in them. Victims are never to blame for someone else's decision to behave criminally or violently. Period. Regardless of what other people, or the media, have told us, it doesn't matter what we said, what we wore, or where we went before someone assaulted or abused us. We were not to blame, and anyone trying to tell us otherwise under the pretext of helping our recovery is not serving us in any way.

Okay, so what role *does* a Fourth Step, or a similar process of examining our past actions, play in our recovery? This is when we look at the rest of our past baggage that is tucked away, those bags that are firmly ours to carry but have been pushed down or otherwise discarded due to pain and embarrassment. We must deal with that shit, because it can hurt us just as much as untreated trauma when left unchecked. Just because we have been harmed by others, that does not give us free rein to harm others. There are lots of hurting people in our lives and in our society, and while we may be able to peel back the layers and appreciate the role trauma plays in our actions, this cannot be allowed to serve as an excuse to behave badly. Why should my pain give me permission to inflict pain upon others? What about my trauma or my suffering gives me that power over another?

We have to start looking at all of our past actions to determine the root source of the action and any harm done, whether only to ourselves or another person. This is hard work. It requires us to fight through our ego to find a place of humility and vulnerability. Our egos want to climb up onto their high horses and proclaim our actions as justified because we were harmed first. I don't know about you, but I believe that an eye for an eye just leaves us all blind. We have to see our actions clearly. We must acknowledge how we dealt with the pain inflicted upon us by others and be brutally honest if we have used that pain as justification for our own bad behavior. As addicts, we are great at doing this. How often do you hear (or say) statements like, "If you had my life, you would drink too," or "If you had been through what I had been through, you would (insert bad behavior here)"?

My Fourth Step inventory was ten pages long, typed, single-spaced, and double-sided. I had a lot of shit to get out. I was not an angel during my addiction. I hurt people. I lied. I stole. I trespassed upon property and people. I had to pull out each moment in my past that I had stuffed down, hid away, or avoided and really analyze it in an emotionally honest way. If I felt my defense mechanisms—such as anger or laughter—kicking in, I had to stop myself and acknowledge what I was doing. I was very fortunate to have an amazing sponsor in my recovery program. She was able to call me on my shit in a loving and compassionate way. This work will require the help of someone you trust and someone who knows you well enough to call you out when you're avoiding something important. Allowing another person into your life in this way also requires extreme trust, humility, and vulnerability—all things we as survivors are not so great at. But if we do it, it will save our lives.

What if the solution to all your problems lay within your own hands, your own mind? This may seem unbelievable after we've gotten so used to other people defining our lives for us. So I'm here to tell you that if you shine a light on a problem, a pain, a feeling, you allow yourself to finally see things clearly. You let your truth in. That newfound clear vision helps us to see whatever you are struggling with for what it *really* is. Then you can deal with it. You can begin to heal the spaces inside of you that have been packed with pain, shame, and trauma and make room for joy, freedom, and happiness. Once you've done this, all of those past choices and actions you were clinging to with shame will no longer hold any power over you. They will become nothing more than trash lying at your feet. Then another thing happens. When you heal, your new light gets brighter and brighter, and others will start taking notice. You will show those around you that healing from even the deepest darkness is possible, and that will give them permission to heal too.

I love the singer P!nk. I love her look, her power, her lyrics. And as I'm writing this, I am reminded of her song "Funhouse." Do me a favor: google the music video, watch it, and listen to the lyrics. It's relevant, I promise. It speaks to the very process I'm explaining to you. In the video, P!nk is dancing among the dark ruins of her life, of her past choices. But the video is colorful, and she is dancing with joy, because she is owning it all unapologetically. She is acknowledging the reality of her mistakes in such an honest and human way. We need to take a lesson from her. Dance with your demons. Dance among the mistakes you've made! *We don't have to be defined by our mistakes.* It's what we do with them that matters. That might sound corny, but it's true. It's okay to fuck up. In fact, if you have a history similar to mine, if you lived for a long time with no access to support or resources, with no other way to cope with pain, hurt, and violence, it's reasonable that you would act unreasonably. I sure did, and in many cases I didn't even realize how unreasonable I was acting until I did this inventory many years later.

In recovery, we begin to learn, we begin to understand, and therefore we no longer can say that we do not know better. When we start to know better, that gives us the ability to do better. We then have an obligation to ourselves and others to use that knowledge to make better choices, and part of that means choosing to heal our own mistakes and not repeat them. If we allow ourselves to hide our mistakes, to not own them and understand them, we will be stuck in that darkness, and we will never know the freedom that true vulnerability can give us.

I do not want to make light of how hard this work can be, but I do want to illustrate for you how freeing it can be. We sometimes tend to intentionally complicate a situation to make it easier for us to avoid it. We make it so complex and hard that it's easier to justify not dealing with it. So let's simplify this whole personal inventory thing, whether you want to call it a Fourth Step or something else. Look at this process as filling up a trash can with all the stuff you no longer need to carry with you: your mistakes, regretful acts, ignorant words, and other times you've hurt yourself or others. Put all that stuff that's cluttering your heart and mind in the garbage, and then release that shit! Take out the trash. If you can, do what P!nk does and dance among the ruins and know that stuff can't hurt you anymore. You now have the power to take all that you learned in your past (the hard way) and create something new. Something better.

This work cannot always be done alone, nor should it be. True humility is exposing our wreckage to another person. It is allowing others to see our imperfections and inviting them behind our walls to really see us. You must find the right person to do that with. That person can be anyone you feel safe with: a victim advocate, a sponsor in a program, a close friend, a therapist, a counselor, a spiritual leader. If you cannot find a person you feel safe with, start with yourself. As I have mentioned already, I had major trust issues in the beginning of my recovery, so I first started unraveling my mistakes and past through writing. I then started finding people who were able to help me, whom I began to trust enough to be able to deal with my shit. I started to realize that trust isn't as scary as I had once thought. Don't get me wrong—it's hard the first few times you do it. As survivors, we have likely had our trust violated in many ways many times before. Opening yourself up to another person is scary, and you always run the risk of getting hurt. But if you don't at least try, you will never know what could have been.

For me, I started by working on trusting myself. Then, as I began to heal, I started to realize there was something greater working in my life: a power, an energy, or a force that was propelling me in the right direction. As I began to make good choices, healthy decisions, things began to slowly work out for me. I'm not saying that everything was easy, but it started to seem like when I did the next right thing, good things happened in my life. Even when "bad" things happened, I was able to look at them and see the benefit, the message, the reason in the situation. Sometimes the message is simply that we have to deal with life on life's terms, and it's not always fair. Sometimes bad and painful things happen without a clear "reason" or "answer." I had to humble myself enough to realize that I was not in charge of the universe. There was a force beyond me working, and I began to trust in that.

If you go to a Twelve Step program, you'll hear this trust referred to as belief in a "Higher Power." And the Twelve Steps themselves refer to it as "God *as we understood Him.*" This terminology turns a lot of people away from these programs before they even start, because they reasonably think the Steps are referring to "God" in a traditional religious sense. But it's not a religious thing, unless you want or need it to be. Your "Higher Power" or "God" can truly be radically different from any religious notion of God. You don't have to use those terms at all. You can also redefine them. Some people say they believe in "GOD" and clarify that to mean "Good Orderly Direction." Your concept of a Higher Power could be celestial and spiritual, or it could just be the understanding that you are not in charge of it all. That's the bottom line here. You don't have to believe in a traditional God or belong to any religion in order to find recovery. What helps is having the understanding that, though you might not know who, what, or whether anything is truly in change of the universe, you are humble enough to know it isn't you. When it comes down to it, believing in something greater than ourselves is a much-needed reality check for our egos. There is nothing worse than someone who thinks the world begins and ends with them. There is no humility when ego is present and active.

Many folks assume that *humility* must involve *humiliation*. That's not the case. Humility is the process of stepping away from your ego and realizing you are not in charge. It does not mean you are weak. It does not mean you cannot be an assertive person. It means you understand your place in the world, that you appreciate equality and boundaries as necessary to create a life for yourself that is helpful and healing.

Access to humility can often be a huge barrier for people in recovery. When we aren't used to being open and honest, it's easy to become arrogant and push away anyone asking us to be humble. It's easy for us to convince ourselves that we are better than this, that we don't need our sponsor or therapist, our family who loves us, or that friend who pushes us to be better because we are different from all of them. They just don't understand what we've been through. Sound familiar? I've had these thoughts, but I've realized that this ego-driven thinking usually leads only to more pain and suffering for myself and anyone near me. My anger rises up to defend my ego. It guards my heart, but it's really just protecting me from vulnerability and humility. My ego immediately thinks that to be humble and vulnerable means that I will be hurt. I will be exposed, and I will be humiliated.

We use this false sense of pride and protection to avoid being open. To avoid being wounded. To avoid moving forward into something that could be perceived as a risk. Herein lies the mistake. If we don't try, how would we ever know? If we don't open ourselves up to something new, how can we ever make forward progress? How will we ever change ourselves for the better? I often struggle with what seems to be a constant battle between war and peace inside of myself. Sometimes it seems like it's programmed into my very cells to respond from a place where I am wicked in wit and savage in tongue. And when you think about it, that makes sense. It's easier to lash out at someone or something that is trying to get you to change than to surrender into softness. I've been practicing this vulnerability thing for a long time, and defensiveness and anger still try to creep in like old friends. What recovery has taught me is that these are moments when I have a choice. It is a choice for me to walk on fire rather than float on water. It's a choice to embrace stability and grace when I encourage the vulnerable side of me and allow light in. When we feel these hard, dark, defensive parts of us rising up, we always have the ability to pause, take a beat, and then decide how to respond.

As an addict and a survivor of sexual assault, I've felt a need for self-preservation and protection all my life. I have never thought I had a choice in my reactions. They always felt so automatic that I never even considered that I might be able to control them if I tried. Now, I know that I can; I can decide how I am going to proceed in any given situation rather than simply just react. There is a quote I love and frequently return to when I'm struggling with this part of my recovery:

> Between stimulus and response, there is a space. In
> that space lies our freedom and our power to choose

our response. In our response lies our growth and
our happiness.

Who said it? I don't know for sure. It has been misattrib-
uted to Viktor Frankl, the psychiatrist and Holocaust survivor.
Some credit motivational author Stephen Covey, but Covey
claims he read it elsewhere first. What matters is that this
way of looking at our actions is so helpful to me, and maybe
it is for you too. Just because I have an automatic thought or
emotional reaction to something, that doesn't mean I have to
act on it. Your thoughts do impact your feelings; the way you
think about something has a strong effect on your attitude and
the lens through which you view the world. But the beauty of
being alive is that we ultimately get to choose how we react.
And over time, we can change our thoughts and feelings as well.

You've probably heard stories of people who used to believe
something very harmful, perhaps belonged to a hateful cult or
organization, and were eventually able to understand why they
were wrong and to change their behavior. Maybe you've gone
through this transformation yourself. As learning, growing be-
ings, we are hopefully frequently checking our assumptions and
prejudices and trying to change dangerous behaviors. A shift
in our perspective can lead to a shift in the way we feel about
what we are now seeing. It can then completely change our
experience of a person, event, or idea. We are more powerful
than we give ourselves credit for. We really do have the power
to change our lives. We have to appreciate the space between
stimulus and response, and we must harness that space to make
better choices, to see things from a different perspective.

The best way I have found to do this is to notice when I'm
having a negative internal reaction to something and then try to
distract myself. Try to replace your negative automatic thought

with something calming, something peaceful. A good memory, a soft melody, one of the positive mantras in this book. Eventually, your brain will start to get it. That thing doesn't have to be scary and stressful anymore.

Meditation is another great tool that I harness in these moments. A lot of people have trouble getting used to meditation. Learning to sit with our thoughts when we've been trying to block them out for so long can be tricky, to say the least. But I think we tend to overcomplicate this valuable tool far too often. I detail the process I use for meditation in the exercise at the end of this chapter. Just give it a try. If you've tried and been disappointed by the results in the past, consider trying it again. You may surprise yourself. I try to meditate when I feel myself getting angry, because I've realized that anger tends to be a mask for my deeper feelings. It's almost never pure anger I'm feeling—it's most often my body's way of trying to protect me from a very deep emotional wound. Feeling anger is easier than allowing myself to be vulnerable and recognize what's really hurting. Meditation is what allows me to access that space between stimulus and response. It gives me the ability to slow my breathing and empty the contents of my head long enough to allow other things to float in and out. It allows me to find stillness. And within the stillness, there lies peace and grounding.

When you change the way you think, you change the way you feel. Period. This realization has been crucial to helping me feel in control of my life after such a long time believing I was completely powerless. I am now able to harness that space between stimulus and response. I can pause, take proper inventory of what I am thinking and how I am feeling and then make a conscious choice of how to act. Here's an example of what I mean:

Old Me:

Stimulus: Person cuts me off in traffic.

Automatic response: "Fuck you, asshole!" My middle finger shoots up as my other hand lays on the horn.

New Me:

Stimulus: Person cuts me off in traffic.

Pause: I stop and squeeze the wheel as the anger rises inside me. I acknowledge the anger, even welcome it, and then I breathe. I try slowing myself down so I can get a handle on the anger until it slowly unravels. I know that if I can do this, if I can harness this moment, I don't need to express that anger. It's not going to help me, and it's not going to help the other driver. I can respond respectfully.

Response: No swearing, no profanity, no horns blowing. I choose to let it go and keep driving.

Now, do I do this perfectly all the time? No. I'm not a robot. Humility means understanding that we are, in fact, human and that humans are inherently imperfect, while also appreciating that we can harness our humanity in a way that allows us to be better. If we harness our humility and allow ourselves to be vulnerable, we can change who we are and how we move in this world. This is such a powerful thing for us as survivors. Anyone who made us feel powerless in the past was wrong. We indeed can master ourselves and change our lives for the better. It just takes humility, vulnerability, and practice.

EXERCISE 1

Think and write about a recent time when you felt yourself becoming defensive. A time when someone wanted you to be vulnerable, and you wanted to put your walls up instead. Then, ask yourself these questions:

- Who are your walls really protecting? Who are you keeping out? What are you containing?
- Does it serve you?
- Does it make you feel good? Happy? Free?
- What do you think would happen if you chose to look inside yourself instead of looking away when you are feeling pain?
- Do you have someone you trust whom you can practice being vulnerable with? If not, start by practicing in your journal.

EXERCISE 2

Let's practice meditation. The best way to meditate is to simply try. Find a quiet place, sit still, close your eyes if you are able, and allow your brain to quiet. If you don't feel safe enough to close your eyes, that's fine too. In that case, find something in the room to focus your eyes on. If you go to a yoga class or do any structured meditation, you may hear the instructor use the term *drishti*. This is a Sanskrit word. In this context, it simply means finding a focal point in the room to gaze upon. This helps with your practice by preventing your eyes from wandering all over the room.

Once you've found a comfortable position, just sit. Be still. Allow emotions to rise and fall in you. You may feel extreme boredom, anxiety, or fear. Try to sit with these feelings, knowing two vital facts: First, they will not hurt you or kill you. Second, they will pass.

You may feel your mind start to spin with thoughts flying in and out. Try to stay still and just observe what your brain is telling you. What thoughts are coming to you? Try to imagine them appearing in thought bubbles above your head, like in a cartoon. Try not to have a reaction to them. They are not real. See if you can just observe them. Listen to them and then let them go. Try visualizing holding each thought bubble by a string.

Hear the thought, and then let go of the string so it floats away. When the next thought comes, do the same. You may experience the same thought over and over. Just keep practicing being still with that thought or image and letting it go. Release the string and watch it float away from you. That is how powerful you are. If you allow yourself to be vulnerable, you can master your own thoughts; you can put yourself in control instead of letting your thoughts and feelings control you.

You may have heard meditation experts talk about meditating for an hour or more per day. Talk about intimidating! You don't have to do that. You may only be able to do this for sixty seconds at first. Guess what? That's great! That's sixty seconds you did not do the day before. Be gentle with yourself. Allow your practice to be what it is. Try not to force more than you are ready for. Set a timer to help you gauge your progress. If this practice makes you too uncomfortable, try using a guided meditation. I use the phone app Insight Timer, but googling "guided meditation" will give you plenty of options to try. You can also try focusing on a mantra, like the one below. Simply repeat this mantra the whole time you are sitting still. Say it over and over again. Allow the words to turn over and over in your head, or speak them aloud. This will keep you focused on the goal of just being.

Meditation

Today, remind yourself of your humanity. You are an imperfect human trying to become the best version of yourself. Vulnerability is the key to understanding where your automatic thoughts come from and how to shift them into understanding.

Mantra

I am not my emotional response.

6

Self-Harm versus Self-Worth

It has been more than two decades now since I created the scars that linger the most, the ones on my wrists that I see on a daily basis and that remind me of the horror, the desperation, and the decision I made to try to end my life. For survivors of sexual violence and addiction, each and every day can be a struggle. For me, my scars are what keep me attached to reality; they remind me daily of my past, where I never want to go again. They also remind me of that day I woke up in the hospital, the first day of my new life.

—BLACKOUT GIRL, PAGE 265

SELF-HARM IS A COMMON WAY that many of us coped with our trauma and addictions in the past. We might have cut or burned ourselves, picked at our skin or pulled our hair, or withheld food, sleep, medications, or other things we needed in order to punish ourselves or distract ourselves from the emotional pain we were carrying. Many of us carry scars, whether visible or invisible to the naked eye, that represent evidence of our use and our self-loathing. Regardless of how these scars were created, they are now a permanent part of who we are. Learning to see and accept them is a vital part of healing and recovery. Maybe your scars aren't directly related to your addictive behaviors. They could be from an accident, a surgery, or something that happened to you when you were a child. You may have physical scars that were left by the person who abused or assaulted you. Every scar tells a story, and many of them carry some kind of trauma. These scars may come from some of the darkest times in our lives, but we now have the power to define their meaning.

My self-harm started shortly after I was raped when I was twelve years old. I was emotionally twisted and had no support or emotional outlet. My parents didn't know how to deal with my trauma—my rape only brought all of their own childhood trauma to the surface. None of us had the smallest idea about how to cope with such intense emotions in a healthy way. One night, it became too much for me to contain within my small body, and I began to have extreme anxiety. I couldn't handle the pain inside, so I attempted to quiet it. I grabbed a bottle of peach schnapps from my parents' readily available liquor cabinet and rummaged through the kitchen cabinets to find a bottle of my mom's Valium and my grandmother's blood pressure pills. I did shot after shot while popping pills into my mouth. I called my mother to tell her what I was doing, my speech slurred. I hung up the phone and attempted to walk over to the sink to grab some water, but my legs were not working. They crumbled beneath me, and I slid onto the floor between our island and sink. The next thing I remember was EMTs coming into the house and carrying me to an ambulance. The lights eliminated my already-blurred vision, and I couldn't see anything. I felt a tube being jammed down my throat, and a nasty taste filled my mouth until I leaned over and puked up black charcoal. Everything went black again.

This suicide attempt landed me in the ICU of our local hospital. I almost died from the medications but managed to survive. When I woke up, my parents told me that I would have to spend some time in the hospital's psychiatric ward because it was deemed that I was a threat to myself. That's where I spent my thirteenth birthday and the following summer. To say that this place was not trauma informed is the understatement of the century. It was like being dropped in the middle of a horror film. I was on a floor of the hospital with one long hallway with rooms on either side. My roommate was another girl who was about six years older than I was. She had long black hair and lay in her bed very quietly. I didn't sleep a wink that first night because all I could hear were the screams of an older woman coming from across the hall. Apparently, she had been resisting treatment all day, and they had put her in four-point restraints. She just wailed all night long.

If you've ever seen the movie *Girl, Interrupted,* that's exactly the type of place I was in, except there weren't only women on my floor. And it wasn't just for teens, either. There were people of all ages and genders. They put everyone together with zero regard for how that would impact us. And impact me, it did. I learned a lot during my summer-long stay. The older patients taught me how to lie to the doctors to get them to leave me alone. I learned how to tongue my meds so I didn't really have to swallow them. I learned the value of various medications—what other patients would give you in exchange. Psychotropics were very valuable. Unfortunately for me, I was only on a low dose of antidepressants, which no one really wanted.

One day, I found my roommate sitting in the shower using a piece of metal she had removed from the eraser of a pencil to make cuts on her stomach. She looked relaxed and peaceful. As my eyes wandered from her face down to the blood swirling into the drain, I screamed. She quickly jumped up, shushed me, and begged me not to say anything. I just starred in horror, and some fascination, at the scene unfolding in front of me. I asked her what she was doing. She replied, "Nothing, I'm fine. Just leave me alone and please don't tell anyone." I spent a lot of time that day just sitting on the floor dumbfounded, thinking about what I had seen.

A few months later, after being released, I sat in my own tiny bathroom lightly dragging a razor blade across my arms and remembering how peaceful my roommate looked slumped down in that shower. That look of serenity on her face provided all the courage I needed to plunge the razor deeper into my own flesh. That's where I learned about self-harm, or *cutting*, as many call it today. It didn't have a formal name back then. Cutting became a part of my dysfunctional survival routine. It gave me a temporary emotional release when I was in pain and didn't have immediate access to a drink or a drug.

It was many years later, shortly after the death of my mother, that I experienced an emotional pain so overwhelming that I used a combination of alcohol and a razor to try to end my life again. That night, I created the scars that still linger on my wrists today. Luckily for me, that night also became my turning point. I woke up in the hospital with a realization that I didn't want to die anymore. My life was worth living, and I needed to get sober and heal my trauma in order to save myself. When I first got clean and sober, I was incredibly embarrassed and filled with shame over the very visible scars on my wrists. For a long time, looking at these scars reminded me of the sickness I held within for so long. They made it clear that I had attempted to take my own life, and I felt that anyone who saw them would judge me as crazy. The only way to hide them was to wear long sleeves, which I did a lot. I would curl the material of the sleeve up over my hand and grasp it to hide the scars. This was before those cool sweatshirts with the thumb hook that easily hide your wrists. Those are made for runners to keep their hands warm, but they sure would have come in handy for me back in the day. Once summer hit and the weather began to get hot, I had to start accepting the fact that I couldn't hide my scars all the time. I used vitamin E and a list of other products on the market that claimed to lessen the appearance of scars. Despite all my attempts, it soon became obvious that only time would slowly flatten the angry raised lines, and completely eliminating them would be impossible. I realized that I had to learn to live with them.

A part of learning to love myself was learning to love my scars. Each day, I made an effort to look down at them and gently trace them with my fingers. Often, I would even kiss them or hug my own arm. These simple, kind acts allowed me to physically love a part of myself that I had previous deemed non-viewable to the world. They allowed me to heal myself. By allowing myself to love my scars, I took the emotional and psychological pain away—I took my power back. The scars no longer scared me. They no longer represented my self-hatred. Instead, they represented a part of my journey to healing, a path from my old life to my new freedom.

• • •

Part of my healing journey included forgiving myself for hurting myself in the first place. I had to give myself permission to let go of my shame, guilt, and anger over the fact that I had harmed myself. I developed an understanding that cutting myself was a negative coping mechanism that I used at a time when I didn't know any better. Looking back on my history of self-harm through the lens of a person who has been clean and sober for so long, it makes perfect sense. Everyone needs something to help them ease pain. When I was a highly traumatized child, no one taught me any healthy coping strategies. All I was left with were temporary fixes for an immediate sensory overload. It didn't matter to me that the fixes I used were actually causing me more harm in the long run. I was blinded by the pain of the present.

For me today, recovery is all about finding alternatives that help rather than hurt. There will always be pain in our lives; that is simply unavoidable. How we deal with pain—that is now squarely in our hands. Do we deal with it by adding more trauma, more pain, more shame, and more layers of guilt upon ourselves? Or do we find things that actually relieve the pain and make us feel like we can breathe again? Herein lies the true freedom that recovery can offer us if we work for it. In early recovery, I learned healthy coping mechanisms that allowed me to deal with my feelings when they came up. This was not an overnight process. Like any major change in my life, it took me time to figure out what worked for me. At first, my main strategy was writing things down, getting them out of my head so they no longer spun around in a shame spiral. Once the words were written down, I then had a responsibility to really look at them and feel what they meant. Feeling was the big challenge. I had to cry, get mad, process my anger, and allow the hurt behind it to be revealed. After doing this, I found that I didn't have a need to turn to drugs or self-harm anymore.

But we can't do this alone. Once in recovery, I was surrounded by amazing people also in recovery who really held me accountable. I would go to a Twelve Step meeting every day in the beginning, which gave me a place to filter my thoughts and my actions. The others in my group helped me understand and appreciate when I was moving backward into old behaviors. The amazing thing about recovery is the community you find when you embrace it. I discovered that there are good people who have been through what I had been through and who are also trying to get better, be better, and do better. If you have yet to find a community of like-minded people who can support you in this way, check out the resources in the back of this book. There are so many options now, whether a Twelve Step program feels right for you or not. We'll also talk more about the importance of community for sexual violence survivors in chapter 10.

If you, like me, do belong to a Twelve Step group, it's important to remember that these groups are intentionally focused on addiction recovery. I don't dive into the details of my assaults and other traumas in Twelve Step meetings. But that's not to say we can't talk about emotional upheaval and how to better process emotions so that we don't feel compelled to hurt ourselves. In the beginning, I found that women's meetings and young people's meetings were often better for me when I wanted to process my feelings. Coed meetings or meetings with people who had a lot more sober time than I did were helpful when I was looking to listen and learn. Something you learn in recovery is that listening can be even more helpful than talking. I could listen to how others dealt with their own stuff, how they processed and were able to heal. I could take what applied to me and let the other stuff just flow in one ear and out the other.

The thing about recovery meetings of any kind is that you have a whole lot of personalities in one room. Sometimes it can be overwhelming. Sometimes it can be downright annoying. Just like in any group, personality dynamics can be challenging. If you can, try several different meetings until you find a few where most of what you hear is productive. I can remember sitting in meetings and wanting to come out of my own skin when certain people spoke. The most important things my sponsors taught me early on were this: Take what applies and let the rest fly. Focus on the message, not the messenger. And most important, some are sicker than others. You have to remember that we all come into recovery because we are highly dysfunctional, engaging in behaviors that were killing us. Not everyone in the rooms of the meetings you attend may be healthy or in a place to give sound advice. This is why it's crucial you find someone who has a lot more time and experience in recovery than you do to be your sponsor. Find someone who sounds like they have what you want. Sit back and listen to people. When you find yourself nodding your head along to someone's story or find yourself surprised and challenged, in a good way, by the things someone is saying, introduce yourself. Twelve Step meetings are an amazing place to exchange knowledge. When you hear something useful, use it.

Besides an appropriate sponsor to mentor us, those of us with addiction and sexual violence histories are often in need of new, healthy friends during early recovery. Twelve Step or other support group meetings are amazing places to find supportive friends. We need people to call upon when we are in pain and find ourselves struggling with what to do with that pain. We need people to help hold us accountable. Often, those who have been through similar things and have successfully made it to the other side are the best friends we can have.

In the beginning of my recovery, I really didn't understand the number of negative coping mechanisms I had. I realized pretty quickly that the cutting, drinking, and drug use were unhealthy and things I needed to avoid. It took much longer to understand that I used people and food to cope as well. I didn't even realize that you *could* use people or food to avoid or cover up feelings. Those lessons came to me slowly through trial and error. I'm not going to sugarcoat this. Recovery from both addiction and sexual trauma is long, hard work. And it requires you to invest in yourself enough to do the work. You have to believe in yourself and your self-worth. And since that isn't easy, I'll go ahead and tell you: *you are worth the work.*

When you make mistakes or slide back into old behaviors— because you will—be willing to forgive yourself. The good news is, each and every action, now and in the future, is an opportunity to learn. When you are committed to recovery, you no longer have the excuse of being so deep in your addictive behaviors that you can't see the impact of your decisions. Being in recovery often feels like walking around with a mirror held in front of you every day. You'll find yourself doing mini inventories on your behaviors all the time. This is what leads to the self-awareness and understanding that will then lead to making better choices.

Part of recovery for me was slowly allowing myself to be proud that I no longer lived a way of life that made me want to die. Over time, I realized that I no longer wanted to harm myself, and I celebrated that. I sought out ways that I could cope with hard things without doing further harm to myself. I sought out other people, places, and things that gave me resources I could use to make better choices. This was hard. There were days when I felt like a complete failure. Some days the shame spiral would come, and I would feel consumed by it. What made all the difference was the slow realization that nothing I was feeling was permanent. None of it would last. I began to understand the emotional current that ran through me—it would come, and it would go. If I could just make the choice not to do anything else to make it worse, the feelings would eventually change. And, ultimately, I would find myself feeling better. When I refused to engage in self-harm, I would not only feel better, but I would also feel proud. I was proud of the fact that I didn't add additional layers of pain on top of what I was already dealing with. And the gratitude that followed that pride would sometimes overwhelm me. I mean, that is *the good shit.* You'll witness yourself exchanging a harmful behavior for a healthy one—concrete evidence that you are changing for the better. And, fuck yeah, you can give yourself credit for that! Celebrate those small wins. Small wins build into big changes in your life.

• • •

So what about those scars the world can see? I made a choice to embrace them. When I was having a particularly hard day in recovery, I would purposefully look down at my wrists and reflect on that day when I tried to take my own life. This always helps to ease whatever I may be going through in that moment because I know I have been through much worse and I have survived. In fact, ever since that next morning, when I decided to commit to a life of recovery, nothing has been so bad, so painful that I have wanted to try to kill myself again. Nothing has left me feeling as desperate and hopeless as I did on that night, and the scars that I now embrace on my wrists are reminders of what I have overcome. I am proud of my scars today. They are reminders of a life I never have to live again. They are tools for my healing. This past year, I chose to get a tattoo on my right wrist, where the scars were the deepest and most visible. I did this as a way of reclaiming that space while still acknowledging what occurred. Now when I look down, I see the pain and the strength that has come from it. You have the power to reclaim your scars too.

EXERCISE

For the next week, practice accepting and loving your scars. Wherever your scars are, find a safe space where you can expose them and see them clearly. If you have physical scars on your body in a place that isn't easy to see, try using a mirror. Once you can see them, take your hand and try to trace them with your fingertip. If you feel comfortable and it's possible to do so, embrace or kiss your scars. If your scars are internal or emotional, visualize them and feel them in whatever way makes sense to you. Take deep breaths and say the mantra below out loud to yourself. Treat your scars as if they were on a small child you were trying to comfort. What would you say to that child who sought your comfort? How would you attempt to ease the pain that child was feeling? Say those things to yourself and to your own scars.

Do this exercise each day this week and then write in your journal about how this makes you feel. Ask yourself these questions:

- Name your feelings. Are you angry, sad, hateful, hopeful, or something else? This can be hard to identify. If you're having trouble naming your feelings, try looking up a list of feelings online. Once you've identified your feelings, explore why you are feeling that way.
- Where is the feeling coming from?
- Is it a helpful feeling or a self-shaming feeling?
- Are you holding on to a feeling attached to your scars?

Allow yourself to feel whatever emotions come up without judgment. If you are sad, allow yourself to cry. If you are angry, allow yourself to scream. If you are happy, allow yourself to smile or laugh.

Meditation

Today, I will not allow my scars to define who I am or how I feel about myself. I will forgive myself. I will not let the person who created my scars control me anymore. My scars will no longer serve as a reminder of my pain but, rather, a reminder of my strength. A reminder of all that I have overcome and endured.

Mantra

I am so sorry that I hurt myself. I forgive myself. I love my body. I love my skin. I love my scars. They are a part of me, but they do not own me. I love myself.

Love and Relationships

Evidence. This is what my twelve-year-old body and favorite
rugby shirt had become. Someone was at my scalp plucking
my hair and placing it into a clear plastic bag. I was so con-
fused, so tired, and ached in places I never knew could ache.
My legs were bruised and bloody as a doctor rolled his stool
in between them to begin inserting a cold metal device into
my tiny vagina; my body began to stiffen and clutch down.
In a matter of twenty-four hours two very different men had
entered my body and soul in two very different but similarly
traumatizing ways. I felt so hollow. So, numb. I closed my
eyes as I endured the last of the exam and drifted off to a
safe place in my mind.

—*BLACKOUT GIRL*, PAGE 16

AT TIMES, I CAN STILL BE SO HARD ON MYSELF. It seems
that, after thirty-some years, I shouldn't still be thinking and feeling so much about that one night I was raped when I was twelve
years old. The thoughts, feelings, memories creep up on me like
a familiar shadow that I wish I could shake off. This event of my
past rises out of the deepest parts of me to the surface of my skin,
and the memory makes me feel itchy, uncomfortable. Just when I
think I have fully embraced and reclaimed my body and my skin,
I am blindsided by a reminder that it will never fully belong to

me. No matter how much I exfoliate, both physically and emotionally, it lingers just beneath the surface, patiently waiting to throw me off guard at my most confident of moments.

I still sit and marvel at the impact one night can have. I think about the fact that one pedophile can commit an act so terrible that it has robbed me of the ability to ever fully be free of his grasp. I spent some time beating myself up over this very feeling the other day. I said things to myself that I often counsel others never to say to a rape survivor. "Why aren't you over this yet?" I ask myself, baffled. "It's been years! It was one event!" Then a gentler voice came and reminded me, "No, it wasn't just one event." It was a night of rape, followed by a retraumatizing trip to the hospital to be examined, followed by having to relive that night to a roomful of people, including the man who violated me, in a court of law. And that was just the first violation in a line of violations that took place over years.

When I step back from those thoughts and look deep inside, I know that what has really stayed with me is the feeling these events precipitated. A feeling that I was merely existing in the shell of my body while having no actual attachment to it. The feeling that I had no choice but to allow all visitors unfettered access to it. It would be years before I would comprehend that my body was mine, not just something to be had. That I held ownership of my body, that I could say no and that others might honor that choice. And even after all this time, I still lose sight of this sometimes. I admit all this to explain why love, relationships, and intimacy can be so complicated for us.

• • •

Intimacy is an elusive concept to most survivors of sexual violence. It's a tangled web of confusion, harm, pleasure, and pain. Sometimes it feels safe like home, and other times it feels like blades driving into our flesh. The challenge of this web is it's impossible to fully disentangle it. And no matter how well we know ourselves, it's never 100 percent possible to predict when an irrational fear will tighten its grip around us. Is healthy love and intimacy even possible for us? I'm here to tell you, yes, it is. I have found it, and it's incredible. I'll explain my long journey toward finding truly healthy love, but first, I want to acknowledge just how difficult it can be.

It is no easy feat to attempt to love someone who has survived sexual violence. There is no printed schedule for the reoccurrence of trauma and no handbook for how our loved ones are supposed to react. Sure, there are plenty of *dos* and *do nots* a person can learn, but no matter how many books your partner reads or counseling sessions they attend, every person and every relationship is different. It *is* possible to fully engage love and intimacy in the aftermath of sexual violence. It takes patience, kindness, understanding, and vigilance. It takes a unique and beautiful human spirit to be willing to stand vigil in the unknown space that we as survivors must navigate. Our allies are vital to our healing. They provide us a safe space to experience, endure, and recover with another person. But we must love and understand ourselves before we invite someone else into our space to do the same. And while it can feel super scary to even think about, it is so worth it.

• • •

Love is not just a feeling. It is an action, a verb, a constant and ever-evolving act on our part and the part of those we love. We have to constantly nurture it to maintain its purity and strength. If you treat love as a feeling, then it is fleeting—just like all other feelings, it will come and go. This is probably why so many people claim to fall in and out of love so freely—they think it's a feeling, a constant engulfment of passion and lust. While those are very valid parts of being in love, they are rarely at the surface of true, sustainable love all the time. More often than not, being in a commitment with another person requires dealing with other, less enjoyable feelings such as grief, loss, pain, suffering, boredom, and yes, sometimes annoyance or downright loathing. These are all feelings—they pass; they rise and fall and come and go. But if love is the undercurrent that carries them all through and out of us, then love remains the bond. A foundation of love, the action, remains intact regardless of the feeling of the moment.

Love is the framework that all feelings about a person will weave in and out of. If you do not truly love the person you are with, then this flow cannot occur. A more challenging feeling will rise in you and eventually release you from any love that was there. This break in the love allows you to engage in behavior that is inconsistent with the action of love. Actions such as cheating, lying, manipulating, or worse—abuse, control, and violence cannot coexist with true love. Anyone who tries to say differently does not understand or respect true love. Their concept of love is not real or authentic. It may not be totally their fault—many people did not witness true unconditional love in their own homes and grew up never learning what it really means. They take what they were taught, fuse it together with their own feelings, and create an understanding of love that gives rise to misguided and sometimes damaging actions. We are all influenced by the environments we grew up in and how we saw love or the absence of it in our own lives.

• • •

I watched my parents sit in a loveless, dysfunctional relationship for the greater part of my childhood. My brothers' understanding of my parents' marriage is vastly different from mine. They both were shocked by my parents' divorce, while I sat there thinking, "It's about time Dad woke up." Funny how five people can live in one house and all have very different perceptions of what's happening. I find that is pretty common in highly dysfunctional families. I would guess this is because we all exist in our own safe places where we construct the reality that helps us get by.

Either way, I saw through my parents' charade pretty early on. I think they were happy once—in fact, I am sure of it. I've seen pictures that show them looking at one another with loving eyes. I know they both "saved" one another from their own dysfunctional home environments. But their own individual demons were greater than the sum of their love, and it wound up destroying whatever joy they had. They were both children of addicted parents, raised in homes that were both emotionally and physically abusive. My father rarely spoke of his adoptive father, and when he did, you could feel a coldness seeping out of every pore. He recalled memories of sitting in his living room bundled up in a snowsuit because there was no heat and nights when his drunken dad would come home and beat the shit out of him. He flinched when he talked, and a shiver ran down my spine when I looked in his eyes. I could tell how deeply his experiences had shaped his view on love, and I can now see how his views shaped me. His pain, his caution, became mine.

I never really felt close to my grandfather, my Pop Pop, even before I knew of the stories my father would tell me. When I started hearing the details of what my father went through, it made me furious. I wanted to lash out and harm this old, nasty man. There was always a red flag in the pit of my stomach when I was around him, keeping me at a safe distance. When I was ten years old, we lived in the same trailer park as he did. After retirement, he decided to become a bus driver—my bus driver. I had to see him twice a day, and I hated every second of it. He was cruel and cut me no slack for being his granddaughter. I was frequently late getting ready in the morning. Being a serious night person with a developing case of insomnia, I hated the mornings. My poor father would fight with me and both my older brothers every morning trying to get us up and ready for school. I was always rushing around the house in a panic, attempting to fix my mile-high '80s hair and get my pink mascara on. Inevitably, I was always running the half mile to the bus stop. There were so many times when I would reach the bottom of the little hill where the bus would pull up, see the other kids boarding the bus, and sprint toward them just in time to see the last person take their seat. Then a smile would creep up on my Pop Pop's face as he pulled the lever and closed the door. He was a cruel bastard who took pleasure in watching me fail. I think he also liked knowing that his unwillingness to let me on the bus would add an additional burden to my father, who would have to rearrange his morning to drive me to school.

It's hard to respect someone who does that, so I had zero respect for him. And since my grandmother put up with his shit for years without standing up for my father, I had little respect for her, either. While I understand there were different expectations back then, wrong is wrong, and I have no respect for a mother who doesn't put her children first. My father's relationship with his mother was severely affected by her decisions as well. He had disdain for her, and it's clear her choices shaped their relationship as adults. My dad never met his biological father. His mother was never married to him, and when she became pregnant, the father wasn't interested in helping with the baby in any way. My father and his biological father never had any relationship whatsoever, and this clearly left my father with abandonment issues.

My father did attempt to find his biological father once when I was a teenager. He wouldn't elaborate too much, but he told me he knew his father's name and discovered that he owned a flower shop called Storm's Flowers in a neighboring town. This was quite ironic because my father's adoptive name was Storm. None of us believed this was a coincidence. I know my dad desperately wanted to reach out to him, but he never did. A couple years later, my dad read his father's obituary in the newspaper. He never went to the funeral or reached out to any of his family. He simply closed the newspaper and in turn closed off a piece of his heart.

I believe I inherited my strength and tolerance for extreme emotional pain from my father. It was from him that I learned not to cry, not to outwardly show pain, as it is seen as a weakness. I learned to be stoic. I have done tremendous emotional work on myself in this area, but even to this day, I feel my father's influence on me. When I'm feeling pain, I have to constantly remind myself that it's okay to be human and to show emotion. It's hard to shake off that armor sometimes.

My mother was even less open about her past. I do know my mother was born in Plymouth, Massachusetts, and was the oldest of what would be four kids by two different men. She was raised by an alcoholic mother who drank a fifth of whiskey a day. They moved to New Jersey, which is where my mother eventually met my father. Information on my mother's father is scarce, as she rarely spoke of him. I have one photo of me at about a year old sitting on his lap. My only real memory of his home is of those colorful hard ribbon candies. He and his wife always had them in a beautiful glass bowl on their coffee table in the living room. Any time I see them now, I get a warm feeling of familiarity. We used to visit him all the time when I was little, but then it stopped abruptly. Their relationship was severed when I was very young, and I was never told why. I just bore witness to the effect it had on my mother.

Her depression grew with each passing year and each holiday that went by without her father in her life. I would often find my mother crying alone in a dark room around the holidays. As a young child, I remember trying to comfort her and tell her how much I loved her. I hated to see her cry, and I remember feeling so sad and helpless that I couldn't make her feel better. I tried to fix her, thinking with the innocence of childhood that if I cleaned my room, hugged her, or was the perfect daughter, surely I could make her feel better. This was me dipping my first toe into enabling and codependency. I was trying to use my positive actions to heal her negative feelings that had nothing to do with me. When it didn't work, I felt like a failure. I took on her emotional trauma as my own, and when I couldn't make it better, I beat myself up for it. This is a dysfunctional cycle that I would re-create in relationships throughout my life.

Seeing my mother crying alone in the dark while never telling me why only reinforced to me that emotions were to be hidden at all costs. It wasn't okay to cry, so it must be done alone in the dark. It wasn't okay to seek comfort from your family when you were in pain. Additionally, I didn't want to burden anyone with my pain when it was clear that my mother's pain was so great. It solidified in my mind that my father's coping mechanism was the right one. If someone asked how I was doing, I would crack a joke or fake a smile and always respond with "I'm fine."

My parents were physically present during my early childhood but emotionally absent. The ripple effects of the childhood abandonment, neglect, and abuse they experienced were embedded in every action my family engaged in. I became an enabling, codependent child as a result. Though there were similarities in the patterns of dysfunction that my parents experienced as children, the effects played out very differently in our home. My mother was good with my brothers—they have fond memories of her. But I had very different experiences. My mother viewed my father as her knight in shining armor. He had swooped in and saved her from her dysfunctional home life, and that made her very devoted to him. When I was born, the last of three children and the only girl, my father was thrilled. After having two boys, my father wanted his third child to be a girl, and he doted on me from the beginning. My mother did not. From a young age, I had the feeling that she resented me for some reason. I could never please her. Looking back with my healthy adult mind, I now understand it perfectly. I was competition. I became the other female in my father's life, and my mother didn't know how to handle it. She became jealous of me, and that jealousy made her treat me differently.

This is sadly not an uncommon phenomenon. You can find plenty of books, articles, and psychological analyses about patterns in mother-daughter relationships if you're interested in learning more. What I know for sure is that my brothers grew up with a very different version of our mother. With them, she was present and loving. With me, she was critical, withholding, and highly judgmental. If I ever got a compliment from my mother, it was always twisted in a way that still made me feel less than. Her love always came at an extreme emotional price for me. It was rarely given freely or without some benefit for herself. I don't think she meant to be as mean to me as she was—her feelings and behaviors were shaped by her upbringing. She was never taught what pure, healthy love looked like. I believe she was unable to fully see the harm she was causing me.

I do believe that my parents tried to demonstrate love for me. I never went to bed without them both hugging and kissing me and saying "I love you." That was a special, important act, and I know that many children with emotionally unhealthy parents don't experience that consistency and effort. It was sometimes very confusing to hear my mom say that she loved me each night after experiencing the way she treated me during the day. Even at that young age, I knew that many of her actions reflected the opposite of love. But because of my parents' commitment to this nightly ritual, I've never had a problem telling someone I love them, openly and out loud. I know this is a gift that not all possess. I credit my parents for that. My issue has never been with saying the words; it has been with understanding what *love* really means.

· · ·

I was about thirteen years old when a boy gave me my first rose—the truest, most iconic sign of love. I remember it well. I was with a bunch of my friends at a roller rink for an all-night skate where half the night we skated and the other half we danced on the rink. Just when the DJ came over the loudspeaker to tell us to remove our skates and prepare for the dance portion of the night, a boy I really liked came up to me and gave me a single red rose with a sprig of baby's breath. I clung to it like it was oxygen. A smile spread across my face like a sunburst on a cloudy day. I lit up that rink like a disco ball. I ran over to my friends on the dance floor and slid down onto the rink on my knees, holding the rose high above my head for all to see. I was high. I was elated. All my friends were oohing and aahing around me, feeding off my energy. Surely this was love. What else could it have been? He bought me a red rose, the universal symbol of love, so of course he loved me.

But a week later he stopped talking to me and was slow skating with a new girl. I was left sitting in my room filled with teenage angst listening to "I Miss You" by Klymaxx on repeat—much to my parents' dismay. That boy and I didn't actually love each other, but that doesn't mean that moment wasn't important and special. There really is nothing like that pure joy of your first glimpse into love before your heart is ever broken. The innocence of the first spark that forms in your belly and makes you feel like you're going to throw up. Where does that go? I wish I could bottle that feeling up and carry it with me as a reminder that it is possible. I have had that spark, that glimmer, a couple times in my adult life, but there is simply nothing like the first. That moment can feel like a drug to some people. Many spend their whole lives trying to recapture that spark and sustain it without even noticing an opportunity for a deeper love when it passes them by.

• • •

In Twelve Step programs, there's an unwritten rule that you should not have any new romantic relationships within the first year of your sobriety. This rule, like many others, comes from the experiences of others who have lived the program and watched and experienced many mistakes over the years. This is good advice. Getting sober after many months or years of addiction is a huge life change. You need time to adjust. As we've talked about throughout this book, healing from both addiction and sexual trauma requires a lot of time and work. You have to rediscover who you really are and who you want to be in the future. Recovery and healing need to be our primary purpose. The focus must be on ourselves, not on another person. If you can follow this rule, I highly recommend it. But I will also concede that it's not always that easy or straightforward.

I'm not going to pretend I'm perfect and own the moral high ground here. I broke this rule myself. I felt it only natural, and almost mandatory, to immediately get into a relationship in rehab. It was all I knew. I was never taught anything about healthy relationships or healthy connection. I found a guy who was just as screwed up as I was, and within two weeks of trading notes in secrecy, we thought we were in love. The women in my therapy group pointed out that this was a bad idea, and I still decided to move in with him soon after I left treatment. Needless to say, that relationship didn't work out.

Now I see that this relationship came from my need for attention. If I wasn't going to use drugs and alcohol anymore, I figured I needed to find something else to fill the void inside. I had no clue how to begin to love myself, so I had to bathe in the false love I got from others. I was still chasing a high. It took me a while in recovery to realize that I could and did use people in the same way I used drugs and alcohol. It's very easy to distract yourself from emotional and spiritual growth when you are solely focused on another person. It's easy to immerse yourself in someone else's life. And the really messed-up thing is, that immersion can mask itself as growth. When you start a new relationship, you feel like you're really connecting with another person. That seems healthy, right? It can feel like progress, but it's really all farce and fallacy. It's almost always an excuse to avoid working on yourself, to avoid actually growing. It's so easy to fall prey to this in early recovery because even the most dedicated person struggles with feelings of acceptance. Everyone wants to be loved.

It's a better idea to spend time alone in the beginning of your recovery, to find yourself first. I learned that the hard way. Focusing on myself was such a foreign concept. But eventually, after being told many times, I realized that cliché about loving yourself first is true. You can't know who you love if you don't know yourself. You can't give love to someone else if you don't have it for yourself. I didn't love myself when I first came into recovery, so how was I supposed to pass on any form of healthy love to another person? All the love I had known throughout my life was riddled with conditions and expectations. There were always strings attached in some way. I was always doing what I thought others wanted me to do, rarely considering what my own heart or soul wanted. I was never alone with my thoughts long enough to be in tune with myself, to know what would truly make me happy. I paraded around thinking I was in love and thinking I was loved when, in reality, I was a puppet on a string.

I'm not even going to talk about my relationships before sobriety. I was in such an unhealthy place that there was no way I could give and receive real love, regardless of the other person or their intentions. After I got sober and started healing, I fell in and out of "love" frequently. Sometimes it was a form of love. Other times it was a distraction that I called love. Sometimes it was hot sex masquerading as love. I have come to know and understand that love has many complex forms. There is love of life, love of self, love of family, love of friends. But the one that baffled me the most for years was romantic love, the partnership love. I would think I'd found it, and then I would wind up bored, realizing the feelings I felt weren't actually true love. Then I would have to end the relationship and cause both of us a lot of pain. Sometimes these relationships were training grounds for what I would ultimately learn about myself and about being in a relationship. This is another reason why it's not fair to date people when you aren't in a good place. Several of my partners became collateral damage in my quest to know myself, to understand what worked and what did not work for me. This wasn't intentional at all or ever done with malicious intent. It was simply due to a lack of appreciation and understanding of myself at the time.

Now, after many hours working on this in therapy, I have grown to understand and love myself to my core. I am independent and have proven to myself time and again that I can take care of myself and be alone. In fact, when looking back, some of the greatest and most peaceful times in my life were spent alone in my small, one-bedroom apartments. I firmly believe that taking this time to be truly independent is essential if we, as people in recovery from both addiction and sexual trauma, want to be able to share our lives with another person. But again, I had to learn this the hard way.

When I started my recovery, I just wanted desperately to be in a relationship. I tried my best to take the lessons I had learned from others and my own experiences and carry them with me into my next relationship. But I still made the same mistakes over and over again. Whenever my heart got involved, my head went out the window. After a relationship ended, I could see clearly why it didn't work. I could articulate all the reasons why the relationship or person I sought was not good for me and tell myself exactly what I needed to do. But when faced with a new person and situation, my heart took over, and I would fumble. I would put the other person first because it felt good in the moment. I allowed guilt and fear of being alone to run the show. I thought that if I dared to be my authentic self and truly put myself first, the person would no longer want me. So I continued to compromise myself and my self-worth for the needs of others. I became a codependent person who fell into the backdrop of her own life for the sake of another's happiness. Just when I thought I knew how to make myself happy, I fell into a trap of committing to a relationship too soon and flailing around in it. Lost and confused, I didn't want to be alone. I could not be alone. I preferred to cuddle up with the wrong person and spend my days in their arms over rolling over to find the other half of the bed still neatly made. The absence of love in my life was too hard to bear. I felt like a failure if I didn't have someone, so I just sprang from relationship to relationship like a dysfunctional trapeze artist.

I picked the wrong people and allowed the wrong people to pick me. I overlooked early warning signs that were clearly red flags of a mismatch. I enabled my partners' unacceptable behaviors out of fear that if I didn't, I would lose them. And of course, if I lost a relationship, that meant I was a loser. I have tolerated enormous amounts of bullshit at the expense of myself. I hurt a lot of people because I didn't take the time to just be alone and process my shit. I thought of a relationship as a symbol to the world that I had made it. "See, I'm in a relationship, so I must be healthy and deserving of love!"

As a person recovering from addiction, I tried to find someone who was also in recovery. This was not easy. Purely thinking about numbers, the number of stable people in recovery from addiction in any given area is small. Add in being a lesbian and, well, talk about shrinking pools of opportunity. But for a while after I got sober, I was so immersed in recovery that I really didn't have an opportunity to know anyone outside of the meetings I went to. I kept myself very insulated within my Twelve Step program, which was really important early on. It was what I needed to do to maintain my recovery. But once I realized that my choices were so limited, I began to date outside of the program. I dated people who could drink normally or socially. I did this for years. I was lucky that my foundation in recovery was solid by that point, and I honestly never wanted to drink again. So I didn't feel the need to drink or use with them. But it certainly was not helpful for me to date people who drank. It was not healthy for me to kiss someone with alcohol on their breath or have it in my home. This I now know. I went in and out of a lot of different relationships. And then, I met the love of my life. And as it often happens, I met her by accident.

. . .

I met Fianne while on vacation with a friend in Aruba. She was from a small town in the Netherlands but had moved to Aruba to take a job as a teacher. The minute my eyes took her in as she walked onto Bugaloe pier, I was entranced. She was beautiful, unlike anyone I had ever seen before. Not only her physical being, but her spirit shone through her in a way that I had never encountered. Her blue eyes danced when she looked at me. She glowed. I was not at all prepared for this encounter. First of all, I was not looking to start dating anyone at the time. I had just ended a relationship with a complete asshole and had zero interest in diving into the dating pool again. Second, I had just gotten off a long plane ride and was wearing an old blue hat with my hair pulled back in a ponytail. I felt grungy, but my friend had insisted that we go to the pier for a quick bite to eat before going to our house. To this day, Fianne still recalls seeing my blue eyes under that hat and feeling an immediate, intense connection. We talked that night. We met up another night to go dancing. Then the house my friend and I were staying in was robbed, and Fianne came to our rescue. Since she spoke the native language on the island, she helped us talk to the police and get a hotel and then spent the next day with us as we tied up loose ends. Then my friend and I unceremoniously flew back home a week earlier than we had planned.

After I left the island, Fianne and I began emailing. That led to Skyping, and then I booked another trip down to Aruba at the tail end of a book tour I was on. She was unlike anyone I had ever met before. She was brutally honest, incredibly kind, confident in a way that could have come off as super cocky if she weren't so pure in her intentions. She refused to sleep with me on my first trip to Aruba, which confounded me beyond belief and intrigued me even more. I had never been with anyone who did not want to immediately have sex. At first, I thought maybe something was wrong with her, but she explained to me that she had been with only a handful of people, that sex was sacred for her, and that I needed to get tested for STDs before we could be intimate. I was like, "What? Who the heck is this chick?" But as the wheels went up on the plane taking me back to the States after that first trip, I wrote on a piece of paper, "I am going to marry this woman." I just shook my head because it was all so wild. But I was right.

This story probably sounds like a fairy tale, and in many ways it really is. But our relationship was and is not perfect, because no authentic, loving relationship is easy or perfect. Especially when one or both of you are bringing the baggage of addiction and sexual trauma with you. But because she is truly the love of my life, we do the hard work. We communicate constantly, incessantly. We argue, we resolve. We go to couples therapy. We have the healthiest relationship I have ever had in my life. It took me a very long time to find this kind of love. I made a lot of mistakes in my recovery and in my quest for love. That is okay. Every turn, every poor judgment, each bad decision allowed me to grow into the woman I needed to be in order to find my wife. And I am blessed. Today, I appreciate that just as my recovery is a journey and not a destination, so is marriage and commitment. A marriage or committed relationship must be worked on each and every day. It is a process. A process filled with amazing discovery, frustration, and intense emotional presence.

My wife—or as I call her, my magical unicorn—can drink normally but chooses not to out of respect for me. She is honest, she is pure, and she is filled with joy in a way that I cannot even begin to comprehend. She has never experienced violence in any form, but she takes the time to research and understand my pain. She wants to love me in the best way she can. She is gentle, she is supportive, and she is all in. She is here for the good, the bad, and the ugly. She does not run away when I put up walls or try to push her away. She leans in, and not in an intrusive way, but in a compassionate way that says, "Have your space, but know that I am here." She is the most refreshing human being I have ever met. She accepts all of me, and she tolerates all my shit—which can be a lot. We in recovery from addiction and sexual trauma are not always the easiest people to be with. Personally, I require a lot. A lot of downtime, a lot of things to help keep me in emotional balance. I am often withdrawn and dark, and she respects that and gives me the space I need. She can also lighten up my darkness in a way that no one else has been able to. She can hold my emotions in her hand and just be still with them, even when they are spiraling like a hurricane around her.

And even though she has not experienced violence, her life has been far from perfect. She had an incredibly abusive mother, and when I look into her eyes, we share a mutual understanding of the harm that has been done. When she is spiraling into her own shame, I am able to hold her, comfort her, and fully appreciate the harm that she has experienced. I hold the same sacred space for her and her feelings as she does for mine. We often laugh at how lucky we are to not have ever shame-spiraled at the same time. It's the universe's way of allowing us to balance one another, I guess.

I say all this not to brag about the love I have found but rather to let you know that this kind of love is possible. I am not unique. You can find this too. It just requires doing a whole lot of work on yourself first and then finding someone who is willing to continue that work with you. I held a lot of people emotionally hostage before I met her. I made a lot of mistakes and went through a lot of unnecessary heartache to get to a place where I found the right person. Remember, *love* is a verb. It requires constant action. A committed relationship is work, and when done right, it can be the most fulfilling work you've ever done. However, self-love is still the greatest love of all. When you love yourself, you open the door to allowing other kinds of love into your life.

My son, Victor, whom my wife and I adopted at the age of two and a half after fostering him since he was six months old, has now given me the gift of knowing love for a child. He has been one of the greatest lessons in love for me. He has taught me so much about love of self and the true nature of selfless love. Much like the Grinch's, my heart grew three sizes the day I met him, and somehow my love for this little dude grows even more every day. He has turned out to be my greatest teacher in self-reflection. He challenges me in ways that constantly test my limits. My love for him requires me to learn how to moderate and self-regulate. I see my own behavior reflected in his words and actions, which is shocking and intense. It pushes me to ensure that he absorbs only the best parts of me and not my worst. He makes me a better human every single day.

Whether you have this kind of love in your life or are still searching for it, know the love you have for yourself must be your first priority. It is a necessary requirement for all other kinds. Take the time to love you. You are worth it.

EXERCISE

How would you define *love*? Try not to overthink this, but write down your first thoughts, feelings, ideas. Does your definition require someone else to be part of the love? Is your definition dependent upon things outside of yourself? Now I want you to think deeply: Are you offering yourself the things you just wrote down? Do you love yourself? If not, how can you begin to explore loving you? What would that require? Once you have accepted love for yourself, think about how you can begin to offer this definition of love to others in your life. How can you deepen the love you have for yourself and others today?

Now make a list of every intimate relationship you have been in; sit with each one for a minute, picture each person, each time frame. What comes up for you? What feelings or memories immediately rise inside of you? Write them down. Are they all different, or is there a common theme, a thread that weaves in and out of each relationship? Explore this a bit as you write, and see if you can discover any patterns of behaviors, either yours or a partner's. Were there things you tolerated that were not safe or healthy? Were there ways you behaved that cause you shame, pain, or anger? Now reflect on what you first wrote about defining *love*. Are the feelings and words you used to describe these relationships similar or vastly different from those you used to describe love?

Meditation

Today, I will choose to communicate fully with the people I love, including myself. I appreciate the role of past relationships in my life and understand that they are not my reality. I can define how I love and how I am loved.

Mantra

Love *is an action verb. I will act with love today and know that I am worthy of love.*

Sex

I wondered why I should even bother using my voice when it didn't make enough noise, use my force when it wasn't strong enough, and express my choice when it was clear I had none.

—*BLACKOUT GIRL*, PAGE 88

I NEED TO TALK ABOUT SEX. I know this subject may be super scary for you—I understand that so very well. As a result of your trauma, you may have decided that sex is no longer something you want in your life. That is okay. You may have never been interested in sex before your trauma and are still not interested today. That is also okay. In fact, there are many valid reasons you may wish to skip this chapter altogether. You may want to skip it now and come back to it later. Do what feels right for you. If you do feel this will be a helpful topic for you to explore right now, let's dive in.

Sex after sexual violence is frightening. When I first started writing this book, I planned to address sex and relationships in the same chapter. But eventually I realized that sex absolutely needed its own chapter. It was not fair nor accurate for me to clump love, relationships, and sex together as though they are different facets of the same thing. They are not. Sex is its own beast for many reasons, and it especially needs to be a separate topic for those of us who have experienced sexual violence.

Sex and love are frequently lumped together in our society. When we were growing up, a lot of the messages we received, from our families or the media, treated sex and love as the same thing. Even as adults, we tend to think they are necessary for each other when they are not. Many poor relationship choices flow from this misconception. You can be extremely sexually attracted to someone without there being any love present. You can have a deep, true love without sex being present. We have to be able to separate these two acts. Healthy sex is just as much of a verb and an action as love is. They can exist together, but they often also exist independent of one another. For those of us who have experienced sexual trauma and addiction, our views of sex and love are often tangled webs that require surgical precision to separate. If we are interested in having healthy sexual relationships, it is vital that we take the time to do this. But it is also super hard and could be unrealistic for a long time for many reasons.

Sex is fraught and convoluted for many of us. I can speak only from my point of view and my experiences, but maybe my feelings will resonate with you. I have used sex in many ways. I have had horrific sexual experiences and empowering ones. During your active addiction, you may have avoided sexual contact at all costs, and drinking and drugging may have helped with that avoidance. Your early recovery time may be wrought with the uncovering and processing of the sexual violence that you have endured, and sex may be the last thing on your mind. Or, like me, you may have engaged in a lot of sexual activity that was not informed or truly consensual.

When I got clean and sober and the haze of my addiction began to lift, my natural hormones began to awaken. I was finally feeling alive in my skin again, and then I was abruptly told to refrain from relationships and sex for the first year. While I believe this is a very important "rule" in recovery, it really isn't super realistic. Most recovery programs don't really address sex or the sexual feelings we may be having in early sobriety. So it's unsurprising that many of us feel the need to figure things out on our own and don't follow this rule. So be gentle with yourself. If you do have sex in your first year, don't beat yourself up for not living up to this rule. None of us are perfect, and this is a journey.

People often say that putting down the drink and the drug is the easy part of addiction recovery. The whole "how to live" thing is where the hard work really comes in. For those of us with histories of sexual violence, rediscovering sex and understanding healthy sexual boundaries may be some of the most challenging work we do. It takes a lot of hard work to fully understand our actions, wants, needs, and desires and get to a healthy, loving place with sex. It is possible. I promise you. It just requires a lot of vulnerability, humility, honesty, and practice.

I think it's almost impossible for anyone just coming into addiction recovery and healing from sexual trauma to have a healthy relationship with sex. It can be especially hard for women, who are often told (whether directly or indirectly) that it is wrong to enjoy sex or that we deserve to be treated as sexual objects. Many of us have been sexually assaulted more than once or have been abused by multiple people. Our history of substance use may have led us to act out sexually in ways that we are not proud of or to do things we never would have done had we not been under the influence. We may have done things sexually for survival and not desire. This is a lot to unpack. I have heard so many people in meetings, especially women, discuss the extreme lengths they went to because of their addictions. More often than not, sex was a major part of that history. But a meeting geared toward addiction recovery is not a safe place to unpack these histories, so many of us are left wondering how, where, and when we can even begin to deal with this stuff.

. . .

Before I started my recovery, I was what society would consider a very "promiscuous" girl. I saw myself as a walking sexual being. I used sex. I spoke of sex often. It was how I sought attention. It was all I knew. This is a very common response to being raped as a child. I am among the one in sixteen women whose first sexual encounter was a rape.[15] When rape or sexual trespass is your first experience with anything sexual, it is very understandable that your whole perception of what sex is will be heavily confused and potentially harmful. Many of us have used sex as a means to get love and affection. We needed to fill that black pit in our souls, and sex translated into attention, affection, and acceptance. In our minds, we mistook that attention for love, and it helped ease our pain. The use of our bodies, with or without our consent, may have been a tool for survival. We may have agreed to sex in order to avoid another kind of physical or emotional harm or even threats of death. Any or all of these past experiences can carry loads of shame, guilt, remorse, or self-loathing into our present.

Many sexual assault survivors say our bodies no longer truly feel like our own. It becomes easier for us to detach from our bodies and surrender our ownership or autonomy than it is to try to reclaim it. So when we engage in sexual behavior, even when it is initiated by us and by choice, it may still not be a positive experience. While we all have different experiences in this area, it's a fact that the majority of people have sexual experiences in their lives that are less than positive. This is not shameful. And if we can take the necessary time to unravel these experiences and learn from them, we can find a healthier relationship with sex.

When I first got sober, I discovered a sexuality within me that I hadn't even realized was there. All of my sexual encounters to that point had involved alcohol or other drugs. Some of them happened during blackouts, some were with my consent, and many were assaults in circumstances where I didn't have any ability to give consent. My views of sex were a mess. I thought sex was something I had to do with men out of a sense of obligation or in search of love and acceptance. Based on my sexual violence history, I figured that if I didn't give it up freely, it would be taken from me anyway. I had evidence that men would do this. One time as a teenager, I did firmly tell a guy no. I yelled and attempted to fight the guy off, but it didn't matter. I wasn't strong enough to stop him, and no one heard my screams. After that, I learned it was easier to just get it over with. That seemed less violent. In my screwed-up rationalization, I thought I was "in control" if I didn't fight off the person trying to have sex with me. If I just submitted or pretended to go along with it, then that meant I was not a victim and it would not cause me harm. I was so wrong. I had no real connection to my body during any sexual encounter I engaged in. I just disconnected. I would detach, which is a very normal response for sexual assault survivors. The fact that I had a choice never entered my mind until well into my early years of recovery. I had intense sexual desire, but most of that sexual desire came from a very unhealthy place, a place of confusion and violence rather than a place of true desire or want.

I knew I was gay at a very early age, but I acted like I was straight for years out of fear of rejection. When I was a child and tried to express my affection for girls in a healthy way, I was repeatedly shamed by adults and peers alike. Being drunk or high made it a whole lot easier to pretend to like guys. I equated sex with acceptance. I thought if I had sex with someone, then that was true intimacy—it meant they loved and accepted me. It meant I connected to someone. It meant I was a good person because someone wanted me.

It never occurred to me that these attachments were based on false narratives I had about love and sex. They weren't real. Now that I know they were smoke screens, it makes sense that they evaporated into thin air. As a child, I had no reason to think I was wrong. So when the smoke cleared and the person or relationship was gone, I was left devastated. I felt rejected and abandoned until I found the next quick, fake connection. I sought out sex not because I enjoyed it, but because it was the only way I felt tethered in an emotional way, and I required that connection. As survivors, we are all coming from very different places in our sexual understanding and comfort levels. As with so many things we've discussed so far, there is no universal experience or path to healing. Talking and thinking about sex and figuring out sexual desires can be really hard even for people who have not been victims of sexual violence. In the United States, as in many other countries, there is a history and culture of valuing sexual purity and innocence and shaming anyone who is open about their sexuality. Although we're starting to become more informed and accepting as a society, many aspects of sex are still considered shameful to explore or speak of, especially for women.

Regardless of what your parents, your teachers, the media, or past partners have told you, I'm here to tell you that we all have a right to sexual agency. This concept is so new to so many of us and can take a long time to fully believe. Having sexual agency means that we all have the ability, the autonomy, and the right to make our own choices about sex. It means you are free to choose. You choose when, where, and how to have sex and with whom you will engage in sexual contact. Knowing this is the first step. Understanding how to exercise this freedom is quite another.

• • •

In order to fully exercise sexual agency, you must understand your own desires and wants. For me, this meant starting with myself. I had to understand that sexual touch did not have to equal fear, harm, obsession, guilt, shame, and all the other negative emotions that had become attached to it for me. I had to start slow. I had to be present, and I had to take note of when and if I detached. If I felt myself detach, that meant I was no longer present or engaged, so I would have to stop. In the beginning, I had to appreciate my own touch on my body. I had to invite it, welcome it, and slowly push through the discomfort to get to a place of understanding my own desires, wants, and needs. Yes, I am talking about masturbation. How else are you going to understand yourself?

I had to really understand desire and where the desire was coming from. The majority of us experience desire and want. As survivors, we need to strip down that desire and understand its source to determine whether it's coming from a healthy or an unhealthy place inside of us—a place that wants attention, love, and affection as a means to feel complete. Taking this perspective required me to really sit with myself and evaluate desire. Was I craving sexual contact—whether with another or myself—because I was turned on and wanted healthy sexual gratification, or was I seeking it for another reason? Was there a gain on the other side of the contact, engagement, or orgasm?

Was I seeking emotional avoidance or pursuing a need to be loved? This process required me to be an observer of my own desires and wants.

It is possible to do this work with a partner, but I would caution you to try it only inside a very trusting long-term relationship with someone who knows and understands your trauma history. No matter how close you are to your partner, having a partner in the mix introduces a host of other considerations that may distract you from the goal of this work, which is discovering yourself. Starting this exploration alone will ensure that it is really only your needs and desires that you are focused on. If just the idea of masturbation makes you uncomfortable, I would ask you to pause and try to dive into why that might be. If it feels like too much of a barrier to get past right now, you can try writing out your feelings in your journal or talking it through with a therapist. It could be that someone in your life convinced you that masturbation is shameful, but that's just not true. If we are attempting to create a feeling of safety around sex and better understand our wants, needs, and desires, shouldn't we do that first with ourselves?

Throughout all my sexual encounters with other people in my addiction and early recovery, I never really knew what my body liked. I rarely had orgasms with men. In fact, there was only one man in the bunch that I actually had one with. So the concept of my own pleasure was super foreign to me. I had to explore different things in order to appreciate what my body responded to and how it responded. For me, I had to do this in a safe place absent a partner. I had to be patient with myself, which was really hard.

Then, when I began to engage in what I would call truly consensual sexual encounters, I still had to learn how to use my voice. It was easy for me to default to old patterns of detaching and just allowing the act to occur. The act of sex was often totally separate from me. This is what often happens when you have experienced sexual violence, when the notion of agency and consent are taken from you. This is a very normal response to a very abnormal event. I want you to remind yourself here: This response is okay. You are okay. You are not broken. You are not dirty, and you are not unworthy.

I had to slowly learn that I had a right to ask for what I wanted. I had a right to enjoy sex. For me, a big part of my healing process was fully realizing I was gay and coming out of the closet. That was a huge step in being true to myself. After my first couple of sexual encounters with women, I started to understand that sex could be this beautiful and wonderful exchange. I started to assert my voice and own my sexual desires. I wound up in a long-term relationship with a woman who did not really have a lot of her own sexual agency, so my journey was not entirely smooth. Once that relationship ended, I began to really explore my sexuality. What I really wanted. Some of the most important sexual experiences for me during that time were with a few partners with whom I had no expectations of love or serious commitment. They allowed me to explore freely.

There's a reason many people think of hate sex and breakup sex as so intense and hot. It's because sex is often derived from a very different feeling than love. It's instinctually selfish rather than vulnerable and fragile. It's often carnivorous, not caring. I learned it was okay to have one or the other or both. We do need to care about our sexual partners. We need to care enough to communicate with them, to listen to them, to make sure everything we do is consensual and serving the pleasure of everyone involved. But we don't need to love them. This romantic myth that love must be present with sex is based on fairy tales about times that were never really emotionally honest.

I'm not saying that a person cannot have both intense passion and deep love during sex, or that it's wrong to aspire to have both. I have experienced both feelings at once, and it is miraculous and magical. When you find someone you truly love, and you share an intense sexual connection with them as well, it's the sweetest of all combinations. It is the holy grail of relationships. But it is also not absolute, necessary, or even possible for everyone to obtain. There are many people who are simply not interested in sex and others with physical and emotional challenges that don't allow them to engage in sexual activity. These people can still find amazing, beautiful love in their lives. Similarly, many who are not interested in romantic love or have not yet found it are able to enjoy wonderful sexual relationships. These may seem like radical statements, but I assure you they are not. They are simply truths. They are the realities of finding your truth and living in it.

For survivors of sexual violence, our experiences and choices around both love and sex are further complicated by our abuse. Things like trust, vulnerability, desire, and intimacy are frequently tainted by past manipulation, pain, and violence. It takes a significant amount of time, healing, self-awareness, and self-love to come to a place where sex and love both can be fully realized in our lives. Some may never be able to experience them fully, and that is okay.

I had to experiment a lot in order to find my own sexual control. There was a point when I had worked at this so hard that I actually went from one extreme to the other. I went from being completely detached and passive during sex to needing to be in control all the time. I felt safe during a sexual encounter only when I was the one initiating and in control. Having no real education in this department, I went with what felt right. I know I was also influenced by what I had seen modeled in my life and in the media. In movies and all other social settings, we're used to seeing sex as this act that just happens. Usually without much conversation. Usually very aggressively. Oftentimes bordering on assault. The images we see are usually heteronormative and portray traditional, unhealthy gender roles. The vast majority of sex scenes in the media show a man asserting sexual control over a woman. He uses his strength or social power to take sex. Very few depictions of sex show conversation, real connection, or consent leading to the act. We are used to seeing a really unhealthy dynamic.

If you are having a sexual relationship with someone, you should talk about sex. Talk about likes and dislikes. Communicate during the experience. When something the other person is doing bothers you, tell them. Likewise, tell them when they do something you really like. It is absurd to think that we just know what everyone wants and likes because we have seen pictures on the internet or these unrealistic scenes on TV or have read about them in romance novels. This is necessary for everyone but especially for those of us who have experienced sexual violence.

It is vital that we understand that our bodies have memories. When we encounter an emotional trigger, those memories come back to us. Sometimes a touch is just a touch, and we can lean into it and feel safe. Sometimes an innocent touch can trigger a memory that is not safe, that immediately leads us to a place where anything that happens next could retraumatize us. This is why we must communicate as best as we can, not just with our partners, but with ourselves.

In the past, I had a lot of trouble interpreting my attractions to people because of the inaccurate and damaging messages I internalized after being raped. I automatically assumed that any connection, click, or attraction to another person meant that sex or intimacy must follow. I am a deeply passionate person when I feel drawn to another. It's not a feeling that happens for me often, but when sexual attraction meets a soul connection for me, it can become overwhelming and intense. I have had this feeling only a handful of times in my life and acted on almost all of them—some with long-term relationships as a result and some with hurtful and very damaging consequences. I was never mature enough or self-aware enough to realize that I needed to dig deeper. I had to look beyond the desire and immediate intense want and actually think about whether the person I was jumping toward was actually someone I should be giving my whole self to in the most intimate of ways. Because of my trauma, sex was all swirled up in my head and my heart as being intrinsically linked with love. If someone expressed attraction toward me, I felt obliged to follow that up with an immediate response. I never realized I had a choice in friendships, in love, or in sex.

When someone expressed interest in me, it hit me as both exciting and scary. Exciting because someone found me desirable, likable, or lovable. Since I had a great need to be seen, wanted, and loved, I immediately responded in kind out of desperation, whether I had reciprocal feelings or not. Then the fear would come and make the whole experience confusing. The fear was based in the reality of my experiences—when people liked me, that meant sex, and sex was not always a choice for me. My experiences of assault taught me that even when I resisted, they persisted, and sex (well, sexual assault) happened whether I relented or not. This made it very difficult for me to determine whether I was truly consenting to sexual encounters. Did I really want sex, or did I agree out of a sense of fear and obligation? Sometimes I agreed to or initiated sex just because I was lonely and craved a sense of belonging. I wanted someone to enter my body, keep me warm, and be in my company for a while to avoid the pit of despair I often felt during those years of addiction and confusion. This is just part of the tangled web of emotions and responses that we have to sort out as survivors.

. . .

I did not fully understand truly healthy sex until I met my wife, Fianne. In the previous chapter, I mentioned the amount of work we have had to do to maintain our healthy, loving relationship. We have had to do a lot of work to find a healthy sexual relationship as well. We have had to do all of the exploration and communication that any two people in a long-term sexual relationship should do. And on top of that, we have had to learn and communicate about how my history of sexual trauma affects our sexual relationship.

Sometimes my wife will just innocently come up behind me and wrap her arms around me. It's a beautiful gesture meant to show her affection for me, and sometimes I reciprocate and can enjoy it. Other times, I will cringe and recoil from her touch. There is no predictable way for me to determine when I'll have that response. It's just part of my reality of being a survivor. After having my sexual agency taken from me so many times, I can react very poorly to sexual and intimate touch. Sometimes my wife initiating sexual or intimate touch can be a trigger for me. When this happens, I have to communicate with myself, in my own head, to quickly assess the situation. I need to tell myself that this is my wife, she is safe, I am safe, and this touch is okay. Then I have to communicate with my wife. This has been the hardest area for us to navigate. It took her a very long time to understand that this reaction was not personal. It was not a rejection of her touch or her love. I had to communicate to her that I was not rejecting her in those moments—my reaction was because a memory had surfaced in my skin. This is hard to communicate and hard to understand, so it took a lot of time and effort for both of us.

On my part, I had to work on relinquishing control, which felt so incredibly wrong to me at first. I had just begun to feel like I had agency in sex: I was in control; I held the power. I consented. But with my wife, I began to recognize all the "I"s in those statements. I had been working so hard to get my power back that I was forgetting that I also had to know how to give it up when I was in a truly safe encounter. In order to experience real intimacy, I had to be vulnerable.

Another feeling I had to examine was my dislike of foreplay. I was never very good at foreplay. Honestly, it bored me. For me, sex was all about getting to the hot and quick act and the orgasm. Once I was with Fianne, I began to realize that this was another intimacy avoidance tactic. I wasn't all super sexually empowered like I thought—I had just become a control freak. To be clear, I'm not saying that I hadn't made huge progress. I had. I could have intense sexual encounters where I was fully present, which was a big feat for me. But I wasn't being totally vulnerable with her, and I wasn't making an effort to understand her needs.

My wife has different sexual priorities than I do. It isn't all about the orgasm for her. Rather, sex is about being intimate and feeling connected. In all honesty, this confounded the fuck out of me. I couldn't understand why she would want to be naked, intimate, and touching each other if it didn't end in an orgasm. Isn't that the whole point? I'm ashamed to admit it, but I judged her harshly in the beginning of our relationship. I thought her different needs were a type of dysfunction in her. How cruel, right? It's my truth and I'm owning it. This disconnect created a wedge between us, and had we not been as committed as we are to each other, this could have easily ended our marriage. We went through long periods without sex because we were so off base with each other that sex was no longer enjoyable. It felt more like work. There were points in our marriage where I considered stepping out and having sex with other people. There were times I would bring up having an open marriage. I didn't recognize it at the time, but now I realize these were emotional cop-outs. I just thought we were too different in the sex department to make it work. Man, was I wrong.

Thankfully, instead, we did the work. We had to dive deep into this in therapy and at home. Our work involved a lot of tough conversations. We had to share our sexual histories and, more important, what we value about sex and intimacy. I had to accept that an orgasm was not necessarily the endgame for her. That doesn't mean she doesn't enjoy it; she does. It's just that the intimacy of being together, being naked, touching each other, holding one another, and engaging in foreplay are more important for her. All of these things require a whole lot of vulnerability and patience—two things I am not necessarily great at, as we have already established. In contrast, the orgasm is more important to me, and I don't always want to spend hours upon hours in bed. Having a child makes this even harder. So we have had to learn to compromise. I have had to accept that if she chooses not to have an orgasm, that is not a failure on my part, and it does not mean she is unfulfilled. I have also had to accept that it's okay to take things slow and be open to intimacy, even if it doesn't involve an orgasm.

This is why it's so important to work through these issues with a partner you really trust. Some people will not have the emotional maturity to understand and accept your trauma and the responses that may come from it. In the past, I have been with partners who would take my trauma responses as a personal rejection or insult to their egos and then proceed to lash out at me. This would only further plummet me into shame and guilt. The lack of understanding and communication in those past relationships did nothing to promote my healing or a deeper connection. You have to find someone you can communicate with, who will be patient, who will listen and understand without judgment. I always thought I needed to be with another survivor, someone who understood my triggers or who experienced similar stuff. In hindsight, that was an ignorant belief. All sexual violence survivors are different. We all have different experiences and different reactions to our experiences, so to assume that another survivor would just "get me" sexually didn't make sense. It's true that other survivors may more easily understand our emotional trauma, which is why support groups and communities can be very helpful. But I shouldn't have assumed that anyone would feel the same or react the same way to sex as I do. What really matters here is the ability to communicate and explore in a safe space. I just had to find someone who was mature enough, patient enough, and compassionate enough to listen and hear me. And I had to get to a place where I was willing to listen and hear her in exchange. Luckily, my wife and I have gotten to that place.

• • •

Regardless of what you have been told, or what you see in the media, there is no one formula for good, healthy sex. Everyone is different. Everyone's body is different, and everyone likes and dislikes different things. For those of us who are survivors, the key to reclaiming our sexual agency lies in honest communication and setting boundaries with ourselves and our partners. We must explore so we know what feels safe and what feels unsafe.

This could mean agreeing on a safe word or safe gesture that gives you both permission to explore while knowing you have the ability to assert yourself when you no longer feel okay. Healthy and wonderful sex after experiencing sexual violence is possible. It can be achieved, and getting to that place is a very personal process. What looks right or feels right for one person is very different from what looks or feels right for another. You have to take the time to really understand yourself. Honor yourself—you're worth it.

When you get to a place of true maturity and empowerment, it should make the sex only more satisfying and intense. After you have put in the work on communication, it can give you the freedom to be vulnerable, to trust, and to be trusted. For far too long, the taboo of speaking about sex openly and honestly has created a culture of confusion and violence. We must eliminate these notions that sex is bad or dirty and has to be shrouded in silence. When we allow these conversations to flow comfortably in our homes, that is when I believe we will begin to really see a reduction in sexual violence and an increase in sexual freedom. Once we remove the shame from talking about sex, we can create space for and understanding of consent, safety, love, and, yes, mind-blowing, wonderful sexual pleasure!

· · ·

If the passion or love you think you have with a person pushes you further away from your true and authentic self, then it's most likely not love you are experiencing. True love should ground you in yourself. It should offer the freedom and space to explore yourself in new, healthy ways. This means being able to be alone, to be separate without being apart. It means being able to do the things you love both with your partner and independent of your partner. It means having the opportunity to spiritually and emotionally grow. It may mean being in an open relationship. Nonmonogamous and polyamorous relationships are more common and accepted today than ever before. If it works for you, then do it. If it feels safe and empowering, then do it. Once we're comfortable communicating about sex, we begin to deeply appreciate how enjoyable it can be. We can have healthy sexual encounters, whether they are fun one-night stands, casual sex with a friend, or loving sex in a marriage or long-term committed relationship. Reject shame and strive for a life rooted in authenticity and self-love.

I have had many sexual partners in my lifetime. I don't regret my sexual explorations because they all taught me something about myself. I often find myself thinking that the concept of monogamy seems insanely out of touch with our human nature and then relishing the safety and comfort of my monogamous relationship. I sometimes find myself wondering, "Will my wife truly be the last person I kiss, touch, and make love to?" For today, that answer is yes. I'm not going to lie and say I never fantasize or think of others in sexual ways; I think that's human nature. The difference for me today is that I have the power to make my own choices. I know I have the freedom to choose, and the intimacy and sex I enjoy with my wife is something I value in my life. So I am choosing that. It is not an obligation; it is not something that I give away or demand anymore out of some sick sense of responsibility or a desire to be loved. This sense of comfort with sex takes time, and I believe it is, in many ways, a lifelong evolution. It changes every day, just as we do. The key is getting to a place where you know that a healthy relationship with sex is possible. It is.

EXERCISE 1

I want you to think back to your first sexual encounter. Dissect it, frame by frame. Was it a positive experience? Or negative? Did it feel safe? Or intrusive? How did it make you feel? How do you think it influenced how you perceive sex? How did it shape your understanding of intimacy? Or love? Write about your thoughts in your journal.

EXERCISE 2

If you feel safe and comfortable, take time to explore your own body. If you feel comfortable enough, do this in front of a mirror. Try to really see your body. Understand and appreciate its beauty. This may be too hard to do at first. That is okay. Be gentle with yourself. I'm asking you to be intimate with you. That's not easy. Take inventory of every touch, sensation, and feeling that arises in you. You may engage this exercise alone or with a partner. If you are with a partner, make sure that they are a safe person. Do not push yourself to do anything you don't feel safe or comfortable doing.

- What touches bring forth pleasure? What brings forth shame or guilt? Write down what you like and what you dislike.
- How do you typically engage in sexual activity? Is it enjoyable? Do you still have feelings of obligation? If you experience negative feelings, write them down in as great of detail as you can.

EXERCISE 3

Close your eyes and think of your ultimate sexual fantasy. Maybe it's a dream you have had and remember. Where are you? Who are you with? What are they doing? What are you doing? What makes this the ultimate experience? Write this down.

Meditation

I will allow myself to explore my sexuality in a way that feels safe for me today. I will not push myself to be anywhere other than where I am right now. While my past sexual encounters are a part of my experience, I can redefine sex for myself and in my life.

Mantra

Sex can be a healthy and loving act for me.

9

Grief

I had no way of knowing how to even begin to grieve the loss of my mother, because I had never really grieved anything in my life. I was used to burying any and all negative feelings so deep inside myself that they could never get out, but this pain was too big to bury. It was too much, and it started to take over my mind, body, and spirit.

—BLACKOUT GIRL, PAGE 165

WE GAIN SO MUCH IN RECOVERY: self-esteem, self-awareness, and new tools to help us cope with past trauma and losses. But it isn't until we are faced with a fresh wound to care for that those new tools and skills are put to the test. No matter how strong and stable our foundation, fresh grief and loss can be devastating blows. Losing someone dear to us can bring up deep feelings of fear and abandonment that we thought we had left in the past. Grieving a major life change can make us feel unstable and uncomfortable and leave us searching for something to ease the pain. Grief and loss make us realize how powerful our tools in recovery can be and must be if we are to continue our path of healing.

When we talk about grief and loss, we often think about death. The death of a loved one can be an incredibly impactful loss. I'm going to talk a lot about how death has affected my life in recovery. But grief can stem from a variety of losses and changes in our life: the loss of a job, the loss of a home, the loss of a friendship or relationship. In the last chapter, we talked a lot about sex and intimacy. So much of my own experience with sex involved grieving. I had to grieve the fact that my sexual experiences were different from those of people who had never been assaulted. I had to grieve that purity. That innocence. In recovery, we all grieve; we grieve a lot. Because we feel. In early recovery, we feel so much that we can feel like walking live wires because we acknowledge instead of running, denying, or hiding in a bottle or drug. Grief is a required part of recovery and healing. We must grieve people, places, things, feelings, and experiences. Sexual violence creates a lot of loss in our lives. Depending on the impact of the loss in your life, grief can last for a long time. However, if we allow ourselves the time and space to truly grieve, healing waits on the other side.

• • •

I was more than ten years clean and sober when I lost one of the most important people in my life, my best friend and cherished sponsor, Magi. It was the first major loss I suffered in recovery, and it impacted me in a very intense way. I walked around in a daze. I went through the motions of my day without really being present, and then I would go home, sit on my couch, stare blankly at the television, and mindlessly eat pint after pint of ice cream. I was numb. I was using food to fill my void. I started pushing everyone away, including Fianne. It was like the pain of losing Magi hit an emergency button inside of me, and all my emotional walls went flying up.

Magi was diagnosed with leukemia in early 2009. I will never forget the day she called me to tell me she was diagnosed.

I was strong for her on the phone, but there was a knowing between us. I hung up the phone and knew my best friend was going to die. I felt it in my gut and in my breaking heart. She had treatment that included a bone marrow transplant from her brother. After that, she had a brief remission that lulled us all into a false sense of security until her cancer came back a month later. She researched some clinical trials and qualified for one at Johns Hopkins that seemed promising. In July 2010, she went to Hershey Medical Center in Pennsylvania for some testing that she had to complete before starting the trial. It was supposed to be a quick stay.

Fianne and I had just met in February and were in a long-distance relationship while she was still teaching in Aruba. In July, Fianne flew over to visit me for two weeks. During that time, I brought Fianne to the hospital to meet Magi. After talking with Magi for a while, Fianne politely excused herself to give us some alone time. When Fianne left the room, Magi looked at me and said, "You need to marry that woman." I already knew that I was going to marry Fianne, and hearing Magi say it after just meeting her only solidified my feelings about her.

Magi never made it out of Hershey Medical. She got sick and died a few days into her stay. We surrounded her with love and ushered her out of this world; I held her hand as she passed. I vividly remember the moment that I knew her spirit was no longer in her body. She was the second person I had watched leave this world, and both times I could feel the moment their spirit left. It's this mystical sensation. I could feel the room fill up with their spirit while the body lay vacant. In both cases, with my mother and with Magi, the body had not completely shut down before I felt the spirit leave. I don't really know what happens beyond, but experiencing those moments has convinced me that there is a beyond.

The last thing Magi said to me was that she loved me. I loved her more than any other human on the planet. Magi was my soul sister; she was that one person I could call and tell anything to, and she just understood. Without explanation, without judgment, she just got me on a cellular level. She was my first call every morning, and she was my first call anytime anything happened in my life, good, bad, or indifferent. She had an amazing spirit and a guiding force that led you to her, a kind of guru energy. She was also gorgeous—like New York City runway model kind of gorgeous. In fact, she did model in New York for a while. But when she got sober, she left that life behind her, escaped a violent marriage, and moved to central Pennsylvania with her two beautiful daughters. We met in an AA meeting and immediately had a connection. She was my north star, and when she died, a part of me died with her.

I became withdrawn and cold. I was bitter and oh so resentful. I just brooded. I no longer had room for Fianne or anyone else who tried to make me feel better. I wanted nothing to do with happiness, and being in a long-distance relationship made it easier to detach. Fianne's radiant light, her joy, was an affront to my pain, and I resented her for having it when it was absent in my life. My need to avoid any joy led me to break up with her on Skype in February 2011. I broke her heart. Thankfully, my recovery was solid enough that I knew a drink or drug would only make matters worse. I was very fortunate not to have the desire to use or pick up. But that all-too-familiar desire to escape led me to bury my feelings in food. I pushed people away and developed a deep, intimate relationship with Ben & Jerry's.

After a few months of this behavior and about twenty pounds of weight gain, I realized that I was not being healthy. I began to reengage in therapy. I increased my meeting attendance, and

I began to write. I went back to the very basics of recovery. To the simple steps that kept me from picking up a drink or drug in the beginning. I began to acknowledge and deal with the pain I was holding inside of me. I talked about it, I cried about it, I wrote about it, and I began to establish heathy eating practices and get my weight back under control. What I discovered during this process was that the disordered eating tendencies I developed in childhood were still lingering inside of me. I had not done enough processing and therapeutic work on this area. Overeating was an old negative coping mechanism that I still picked up when things got a bit unmanageable in my life. My grief led me to better know myself.

In April, as I was emerging from this mess, I looked Fianne up on Facebook. She had unfriended me, and we had not spoken since I dumped her, but I just wanted to see how she was. I saw she was celebrating her birthday. She posted a photo of herself with another blonde, with their hands touching ever so slightly. My heart fell into my shoes. I thought she had already moved on and I had lost my chance with this beautiful butterfly of a person. I took a deep breath and emailed her to apologize. I was not proud of what I had done. It was pure survival. I tried my best to explain what I had been going through and why I could not be in her presence. Thankfully, she was receptive and open to talking to me, and we emailed back and forth. Then we Skyped, and I slowly began to heal the harm I had done. She was not in a relationship with anyone—the person in the photo was just a good friend. She told me she had been miserable and missing me. I flew to Aruba to see her, and we have not been apart since—although she will still often remind me of that one time I dumped her.

. . .

Most recently, I lost my father to cancer. He was diagnosed in August 2016. I will never forget the day I realized something was deeply wrong. He and my stepmother, Pat, had been away for two weeks in Maryland, so I hadn't seen them in a while. We were meeting for dinner at one of our favorite cheesesteak joints, and as soon as he sat down and took off his coat, I saw that his arms looked so frail. He had clearly lost at least ten pounds since I had seen him last. My eyes flew from his arm to my stepmother's face, and I said, "What is going on?" She shook her head. They both explained that he wasn't feeling great and they had made an appointment with the doctor. They were supposed to travel soon to a beach in Maine with me, Fianne, and our two foster children at the time, Tea and Victor. They canceled, and I cried every day of the trip. Like the feeling I'd had with Magi, I simply knew that I was losing my dad. I knew he was going to die.

I walked with him through his short battle with cancer. I went with him to almost every doctor's appointment and his weekly chemo treatments at the veterans hospital. My father was a first infantry Vietnam veteran who had seen more than anyone should have to by the time he was twenty-five. No doubt the cancer coursing through his veins was a direct result of the Agent Orange doused upon our soldiers during that war. Agent Orange was a tactical herbicide the US government sprayed in Vietnam from 1961 to 1971 in an attempt to clear the trees of their leaves so our soldiers could see the enemy approaching. Like much of that war, all it did was further harm our American soldiers. Many of them died. Those who came home were treated like shit only to learn later in life that the herbicide was causing all kinds of medical issues that were killing them. There are more than fourteen diseases that we now know can be caused by Agent Orange—lung cancer, the disease that killed my father, is among them.

He died on January 6, 2017, surrounded by my stepmother, my niece, and me. Again, I had the mystical experience of watching a spirit leaving a body. It was and continues to be the most painful experience of my life. My father was my rock, and I was not ready for him to go. I still get very angry sometimes thinking about how unfair it is that he's no longer here. Adjusting to life after losing both parents is a very odd process. You lose your past. All my grandparents are gone as well, and I realized one day that I no longer have anyone to go to with questions about my life, my family's history, and my past. It was a scary and strange revelation.

I am very grateful that my father got to see me clean and sober for more than twenty years. He and I had an amazing relationship over that time, but I wanted and still want more time with him. Loss is hard. But I was able to learn from the mistakes I made after losing Magi. I dealt with the loss of my father differently—I fully embraced the pain. I was more mature about my grief. I didn't try to avoid it or run from it this time. It felt almost disrespectful to my father to deal with it in any other way. He deserved more than that from me. I remember just lying with his body while waiting for the coroner to come to the house. I helped the hospice nurse clean him and dress him. When the coroner arrived, I stayed in the room and helped him wrap my father up and carry him out to the hearse; then I watched them drive away with him. I didn't want him to be alone. It felt like a true honor to be able to do that. My father had always wanted to be cremated. He used to joke that when it was time for him to be cremated, someone better make sure his ass was really dead. He was funny like that, always cracking jokes that would seem totally inappropriate to many. But for us, that was just my dad. I took this to heart. I called the coroner and asked if I could accompany him to my father's cremation.

The coroner didn't flinch and said of course I could. My brothers and stepmother didn't understand my need to do this, and that's okay. It was something I needed to do for my dad. It felt like a promise I needed to keep.

The day after he died, I was sleeping on the couch at my parents' house when I awoke suddenly. A rush of air filled my lungs, my body bolted upright, and my eyes opened. In that moment, I saw my father's face appear in front of me. His face just hung in the air. No body. Just his face and his beautiful blue eyes looking into mine. He was no longer sick; it was my father in a healthy form. His face was full, his smile was huge, and his eyes were as warm as I had always known them to be. I just stared at him. And then as quickly as he appeared, he was gone, and I was left with this overwhelming sense of peace. I know this sounds insane, but I swear on everything I am that this happened. I was not hallucinating, and I was not dreaming. I could feel him. I knew he was still there in my presence, offering comfort and love. I lay back down on the couch and fell back to sleep. I woke up the next day unsure if I should say anything to the rest of my family. I eventually did tell them. I think that was my dad's way of letting me know that he was okay and that he was with me. So as Fianne and I drove to the crematory, I said jokingly to him aloud, "I will be with you to the end too."

The crematory was this little nondescript shedlike building in Mount Joy, Pennsylvania. You would never know what it was from the outside. The staff at the funeral home we used were so incredibly sweet and supportive, and they didn't make me feel weird or morbid for being there. They got it. They carried the box that held my father's body into the cremation chamber. I asked them to open it so I could see him one last time. I told them about my father's joke, and I said I have to make sure he's dead before he goes in. I saw my dad's face one more time; it was very pale. As I leaned down and kissed his cold forehead, I said, "Just making sure, Pop." I smiled through my tears because I knew he was laughing. I closed the box, and one of the staff members told me I could hit the two buttons that started the process of igniting the furnace and slowly carrying him into the chamber. The whole process of reducing the body to ashes takes several hours. I didn't stay that whole time, but I'm glad I was there and was able to see how it all happens. It felt right to be with him—or rather, his body—until the very end. I was never in the military, but I have great respect for the notion of not leaving anyone behind. My father was not just a soldier in the United States Army; he was my soldier in life. He never left my side; he was there for it all. Ever present, through the shit, the joys, and the pains. I felt like it was my duty to guard him to the end as well. It felt like such an important way for me to honor him and all of his sacrifices.

When it came time to properly grieve my father's death, there was no way I was going to allow myself to cop out and make excuses. I allowed myself to feel all the feelings I needed to feel each day. I faced each day of this new grief with a better understanding of how to cope. I still speak of him often and cry openly when the feelings arise, and I did not retreat into eating or other negative coping mechanisms after his death. I allowed myself space to grieve, heal, and feel. While the pain of losing my dad has been the greatest I've ever felt, I have also coped with it in a healthier way than I've dealt with any other grief or loss. I feel like that was the final gift we gave each other. I dealt with his death in a raw, honest, and brutally present way. He deserved that from me. And in return, he taught me that this healthy process of grieving is possible.

• • •

The death of a loved one is just one very potent kind of loss and grief we may experience in recovery. Recovering from addiction brings a whole host of losses in and of itself. We must grieve the person we thought we were; we grieve the friends and places we used to associate with that are no longer healthy for us. We grieve a lifestyle that we can no longer have, and we must grieve the drink or drug that was our constant companion. We must acknowledge that, as addicts, we are built differently. We can't have just one glass of wine at dinner or one beer at the game. We can't just smoke one joint or do one line. Thankfully, that sank in with me early in my recovery. I was laughing even as I just typed those words because I never, ever, in a million fucking years, ever had just one. I had to really process the fact that I was different. I had used up my drink tickets early in life, and those things were no longer accessible to me if I wanted to continue down a path of healing. There have been times in my life when people have come up to me and said things like, "But you've processed your trauma now. You don't think you could have just one drink?"

To this I reply, "No, because I never could have just one drink." The first time I drank at age twelve, I drank alcoholically. This was before the layers upon layers of trauma entered my life. I am an alcoholic. For whatever reason, my chemistry does not process alcohol the same way other people's chemistry does. I cannot just have one or two drinks. Do I see a martini glass sometimes and fantasize about having one? Yeah, I'm human. But when I really process it, it's not the alcohol that I want. I'm actually fantasizing about the glamour it signi- fies in our culture. The pretty glass, the false sophistication that holding it at a bar or social gathering provides. And yes, there are times when I am sick and tired of being the proper, moral, sober person all the time. I'm not going to lie. Alcohol gives people a free pass to act badly. It's often used as a social permission slip to engage in behavior that people normally would not have the balls to do sober. It becomes a socially acceptable excuse to fuck up. People are much more forgiving toward bad behavior when someone is hammered. They understand it and they can relate to it, so it often goes less punished. Trust me, sometimes I would love to cut my losses and be able to use that free pass. But then I remember I am not a normal drinker. Never have been.

When I put alcohol into my system, I cannot stop. Something inside takes over, and I lose all ability to control my consumption. I will drink in excess, and then I will lose myself. I will most likely act like a total asshole, offend people by saying things I do not mean, do things I would never do with a clean head, and wake up the next day with a horrific headache, stomach rot, and a boatload of shame and required apologies. This does not sound like a good time. This is not a chance I want to take. No thank you. So anytime I think, "Oh, I could just have one . . ." I stop myself and I remind myself that I'm simply not built that way. Suppose you had an allergy to something, like shellfish. If you knew that if you ate just one or two shrimp, your throat would close up and you would wind up in the emergency room or worse. You would probably avoid shrimp, right? Yeah. Alcohol is my shrimp. Nothing good comes from having it, and it literally could lead to my death. If I doubt that for a second, I just have to look at the damage I did to myself the last time I drank. I look down at my wrists and realize nothing is worth that. I look around at my home, my family, and the life I have built for myself, and nothing is worth setting fire to all of that. The outcome of that "one drink" for me could literally cost me everything. And for what? Social comfort? A good time? The ability to shift my bad behavior onto alcohol in order to let loose for one night? No thank you. Not worth it. Not even a little bit. Finding my true self, committing to a healthy, sober, recovering life, was one long grieving process.

As I've mentioned, coming to terms with my history of sexual violence also involved a lot of grieving. I had to grieve the innocence of my childhood that was raped from me. I had to deal with the feeling that my body had been taken from me and figure out a way to be comfortable in my skin again. I had to learn how to allow touch, hugs, and intimacy into my life without them bringing forth feelings of suffering. That was a whole grieving process unto itself, and it took a very long time. Hell, it still rears its ugly head at times. But because I have done the work, when I do feel those sharp moments of loss, it's more like a quick glitch rather than a huge setback.

Much of my grieving process related to sexual trauma took place in the bathtub. The bath was the one place I felt truly free to let my walls down and open myself up to grieving and feeling. In early sobriety, I developed a whole bathtub ritual that engaged all my senses. I would fill the tub with hot water and add some scented oil like lavender or ylang-ylang. I would play heart-wrenching music like Sarah McLachlan to open myself up to sadness. I would light tons of candles so I had the soft glow of fire surrounding me. Then, I would sink into that water and allow all the sounds and smells to engulf me.

In the beginning, this was how I accessed my vulnerability enough to begin to grieve. To cry, to scream, to hold myself, to masturbate, and to explore all of my feelings safely. If the porcelain walls of my bathtubs could talk, they could write their own memoir. But truly, this is where I did so much of that hard work I've talked about. I found a place that felt safe enough, and I went there often. That gave me the necessary time, space, and freedom to grieve and heal. To fall apart and put myself back together.

I had to acknowledge everything I was giving up, accept it as a loss, and then process it properly. Thinking about those moments in the bathtub still conjures up warm feelings for me. And for recovering people, reminders of our many losses can come up for us at any time, without warning. So it's very important to find our safe places to process. We must create rituals and spaces in our lives where we can safely do this hard work. Places we can retreat to when those daily reminders emerge. When a new experience enters our lives and requires us to experience loss—which will happen—that's life. We must remember we can walk through it. It will not destroy us or take us back into a bad place if we acknowledge it and if we allow ourselves the time and space necessary to properly grieve.

• • •

For me, grief is like this heavy quilt that sits upon my shoulders, wraps around my chest, and makes it hard to catch my breath. Grief weighs you down and makes standing tall a monumental task. It can be so heavy that you feel like you cannot get out of bed and walk through the day. You cannot run from grief; it will follow you wherever you go. But if you understand it, it becomes easier to bear. If you embrace it, you can walk a bit taller and allow yourself to surrender when you need to retreat inward to find healing. It must be felt and processed for it to find its way out of your skin. Some days are better than others. In fact, you can walk around all day and almost forget that you are grieving. But then something always comes up to remind you. A familiar smell, location, or TV show jogs a memory that brings your mind right back into the raw and real pain of your loss. As the days go by, these moments may become less frequent, but they never truly go away. The best way to cope is to allow yourself the freedom to fully embrace the emotions that rise in you.

Personally, anger is a big part of my grief. They go hand in hand. I like to remember that anger is just sad's bodyguard, so it makes sense that anger is deeply involved in my grief experience. Anger acts like strength, but it is weak in form; it lacks structure and depth. It's shallow. It's ego. It's vanity at its worst. I was angry for a really long time at the beginning of my recovery, and much of that anger was righteous. It was justified anger against the people who abused me or allowed it to happen. But at some point, I had to realize it was also bullshit. It was my way of avoiding my deeper feelings.

Real strength, real power is lightness of heart, vulnerability rooted in self-awareness. It takes more strength, more courage, and more power to choose the kinder path. To lower your voice and release your furrowed brow. Real power comes from deep within, when we can choose to love and show compassion rather than lash out in fear and cowardice. Anger is nothing but fear. Putting up walls in the name of self-care is utter bullshit. It does not serve you or others. It offers you nothing but despair. If we allow ourselves to relinquish our fierce grasp on fear and self-protection, we can open ourselves up to love. To kindness. To healing.

Our emotions are like the ocean, ever changing. When the tide comes in, it must also retreat again. It's the yin and yang of life. No one feeling or emotion will stay with you all the time. Knowing this makes it easier to deal with the rough undertow of grief when it pulls you under. Just as there is dark, there must be light. When you are abruptly brought back into a dark place of pain and grief, remember that it is only temporary. Grief is purposeful. It helps us gain a deeper understanding of the pain that we all experience in life. After a period of grief, we can come back into the light even stronger. And we'll be much more prepared when the next tide comes.

· · ·

One of the most important lessons I learned in recovery was to suit up and show up. Sometimes, the most important thing you can do on any given day is to simply get out of bed and face the day. Be present amid the pain and allow yourself to grieve. It's a start. It is forward motion. That does not mean the rest of your day is going to be easy or without pain and suffering. It just means you have chosen to face it rather than avoid it and run. Understanding that there is a light above and there will soon be calmer waters in your mind, body, and spirit can be comforting. We cannot always predict when these emotions will rise to the surface. But to prepare ourselves, we can remember that feelings aren't facts. We can harness our feelings to bring us into a deeper and more meaningful understanding of whatever we are grieving. But you must do the work; you must go through the pain in order to get to the other side of it.

Grief will always be present in life. No one's life is without loss and pain. But all the work we do on our recovery from addiction and sexual trauma will also help us meet grief with compassion and understanding when it arrives. We will be open to healing our pains, which means openly and honestly grieving what we have lost and will lose in the future. This evolution has been truly transformative for me. I now know that I can face anything. No loss, no pain can destroy me and the healthy life I have built. Today, I have the tools necessary to face grief and walk through it, and so can you.

EXERCISE

For me, the bathtub was a place where I felt safe to be vulnerable. Do you have a safe space where you can really open up and feel your grief? Make a list of places where you feel safe enough to be vulnerable. If nothing immediately comes to mind, think of times you feel peaceful. Maybe it's by the ocean listening to waves crashing against the shore; maybe it's on a hike through a thick forest; maybe it's while riding fast on a bike or during meditation or prayer. See if you can establish a ritual or create a space that allows you to access your grief in a safe way. If you need to prepare a space to make it safer, take the time to do that. Set aside regular time in your schedule to spend at a yoga class or in your place of worship. Go to this place and practice giving yourself the time to release the grief out of your mind, body, and soul. You may be amazed at how much lighter you feel.

Meditation

Today, I will fully embrace all emotions that rise inside of me. I will cry if I need to cry, scream if I need to scream, and laugh when I need to laugh. I will allow myself the freedom to process my grief in a healthy and loving way. My pain will not determine my experience. I can walk through grief with strength and grace.

Mantra

My feelings aren't facts. I will be gentle with myself and fully feel the grief that rises and retreats inside me. I will trust this process, as hard as it can be, because I know it will not last forever.

10

The Survivor Connection

Every single time I speak publicly, a survivor, or two, or three, or four approach me afterwards to share their own story. Oftentimes, they tell me I was the first person they had ever told. Personal healing starts when we feel connected to another, when we feel less alone and we know that our experiences—while horrific and deeply personal—are shared.

—BLACKOUT GIRL, PAGE xvii

MY EYES FLY OPEN AS MY MIND SPIRALS in a million directions. Sleep is elusive, as it usually is the night before a big event in my life. In several hours, I am scheduled to give a huge speech on my own story as a survivor of sexual violence and the importance of loosening legal constraints that shorten the amount of time during which victims and survivors of sexual violence may come forward with their experiences.

A statute of limitations is a law that states a certain crime must be reported within a certain time frame of its occurrence in order to bring charges against the perpetrator. These laws are meant to protect defendants, but they are not based in any science or knowledge of how a victim actually processes a crime as traumatizing as sexual assault. There is no science that says five, ten, or fifteen years is long enough for a person to heal or that these time frames have any impact on a sexual predator's behavior or likelihood to reoffend. The truth is that delayed disclosure is actually the norm, not the outlier, in sexual assault cases.[16] Survivors need time to heal and come forward. And laws that prevent victims from filing charges after an arbitrary period of time allow rapists to continue walking free, further endangering their victims and the general public.

After hearing all of this from survivors and advocates, many states have begun to reform or eliminate the statute of limitations for rape cases. In recent years, the Jerry Sandusky case, the Bill Cosby case, and the grand jury reports on Catholic clergy abuse have put Pennsylvania's sexual violence laws in the national and international spotlight. In particular, the investigations of Catholic clergy revealed that the cover-up of the abuse of children involved everyone in the church's hierarchy, including the Vatican in Rome. It opened wounds all over the world as more and more survivors came forward to share their stories. One of the glaring issues that came out of these cases was that the statute of limitations had expired for many victims. The grand jury report showed how Catholic Church officials explicitly used this to their advantage, calculating the statute of limitations on the crimes they were aware of before doing their legal duty and reporting the crimes to law enforcement. It was and still is the single most egregious depiction of systematic abuse and cover-up in our history.

Those of us working with victims and survivors have known the dangers of this system for decades, and we have been fighting for reforms to our state laws to abolish the time constraints on sexual assault. I have been working with victims and survivors of sexual assault for close to twenty years, and a core group of about twenty-five of us have kept in constant communication. We update each other on the status of bills, help with media interviews, and provide emotional support and encouragement. We have become somewhat of a family, storming the capitol, holding rallies, meeting with legislators, and demanding collective change to our laws to help other survivors. On this morning, when I woke up at 2 a.m. and I couldn't get back to sleep, I went onto our group chat and sent out a message about my event and my anxieties. Within seconds, my phone began buzzing with replies. A flurry of messages came across my screen, all with nothing but unconditional love, support, and understanding. For a variety of reasons, across the time zones, many were also awake dealing with their own anxieties, realities, and lives. What I felt was that sense of connection, that we were all in the same boat, sending out encouraging messages in a time of need for one that became a time of need for all. I felt that I was a part of something, and my anxiety eased a bit.

This is what having a survivor connection feels like. You feel seen, heard, and understood. When you can find other people who have been through similar situations, you find your people. And if you're lucky, you find a family. In my group, we all come from very different backgrounds, and all of our stories are unique. But we were all victims of sexual violence, and we are all living in its aftermath in our own ways. We are at vastly different places on our healing journeys, and we don't always agree. But this common thread that binds us is one of the strongest bonds I have ever experienced. When you meet another survivor, there is often a knowing between you. Something in their eyes feels and looks familiar. I see it often.

• • •

When I'm touring and speaking, there are always those moments when my eyes will lock with someone's in the audience, and I see that look. I see that person communicating their truth as I am exposing mine. I see the recognition and, in most instances, the relief. Having that shared moment is powerful and comforting. When you walk into a support meeting for those struggling with addiction, there is often a feeling of belonging, a sense of home. The same goes for survivors. There is a reason that peer-support groups have worked for decades. When two people come together with a similar purpose or bond and share their experience, strength, and hope with each other, they create space for connection and understanding. They create space for healing.

One of the hardest parts of being a survivor of sexual violence is living in silence and secrecy. Far too many of us have suffered silently thinking we were the only ones. We deeply believe that no one could ever understand the depths of our pain. Our perpetrators, our friends and family, and our sense of self-preservation all tell us that we have to keep quiet. And the media and justice system show us that if we do speak our truth, no one will believe us. This loneliness can be debilitating. But in the last few years, we have started to see a shift. People have started to speak up. We are starting to see the reality that there was an underground army of us just waiting for our moment. Slowly, this ripple effect gave way to a current that became a wave that has crashed over our society as story after story has come to light. More and more people are finally feeling able to step into that light and see, truly see for the first time, the reality of sexual violence and what it has done to us. Survivors are uniting in truly magnificent and bravely public ways. Between the Sandusky survivors, the Cosby and Weinstein survivors, the R. Kelly survivors, the survivors of abuse by Catholic clergy, and all others who have come forth with revelations big and small, local and national and international, our stories have been recognized in every magazine, news outlet, and social media site. People are coming together. They are marching.

They are standing in solidarity, and it's freeing. And for many, it's also paralyzing.

Breaking that silence is scary and can even create a new layer of loneliness. I would contend that there is no other violation like sexual violence. In this book, we've talked about so many ways it leaves an undeniable mark that cannot be seen by the naked eye. It lives in us and comes out in us. It's very hard for people who have *not* experienced sexual violence to understand our pain, our fears, our ways of moving through the world while carrying the weight of this experience every day. But when we meet other survivors and discover that we are a little less alone in this world, that can be transformative. In order to get through the day-to-day struggles we all face as survivors and people in recovery, we need each other. We need to be able to find that connection to another person and a community. Some people find that by speaking up in a public setting. For others, this feels impossible and even more traumatizing, and that's okay. No one needs to report their assaults or speak up publicly in order to find healing after sexual violence. For so many survivors, just admitting it to themselves is enough. Maybe for you, it was the act of picking up this book and allowing yourself the space and time to read it. This #MeToo era we're living in is wonderful for so many who want to publicly acknowledge what they have been through. But seeing these stories and feeling like you cannot share yours in the same way can also feel very isolating. I will assure you, you do not have to be public about your assault for your story to be valid. You do not need to rush to a podium or pick up a rally sign exposing your experience in order to heal and be a part of this movement. The quiet recognition and reconciliation in your own life can be equally empowering and vital to not just your own healing but the healing of our society. Please try not to compare your reaction, response, and healing to anyone else's. Your process is yours. Period.

• • •

The antidote to loneliness is human connection. Just like water and air, as humans, we require a sense of belonging. We are not meant to walk through this human experience alone. We are meant to connect with others. To bond. Connection to others allows us to feel less alone; it creates happiness, security, and acceptance. These are key elements to managing life on life's terms. We need each other to be there. And we can't share this kind of connection with someone who doesn't understand us. We need connections with people who have gone through what we have gone through, have come out the other side, and can share their wisdom. We need connections with people who will validate us and honestly say, "I understand," when our pain feels inescapable. We need to be able to pick up the phone and text or call someone who just gets us. Who accepts us.

When I sent that message out to my community of survivors and my phone lit up in response, I immediately felt better. I felt understood. I felt less alone. I felt like I could get through that day. I felt like less of a freak for being wide awake at 2 a.m. because my people were also wide awake dealing with unique but similar issues. When we reach out, we enable a vital safety net in a life of long-term recovery. Don't get me wrong: reaching out and asking for help can be *hard*. It may be hard because we've done it in the past and been ignored or worse. And it is hard because it requires us to do the other things we've talked about: be vulnerable and be honest. But if we can find our people and if we can work up the courage to reach out, we will have another amazing tool for healing and recovery. We cannot do this alone, and the beauty is, we don't have to.

· · ·

So how do you find your people? How do you find the folks who really get you? You will have to put yourself out there a bit. There are many resources online. Check out the resources and organizations at the back of this book. There are tons of online chat groups and in-person support groups. Some are hosted by nonprofit agencies that do this work, whether rape crisis programs, victim service agencies, mental health agencies, or suicide prevention organizations. Search online for any of these types of programs, and you will find online chat groups and ways to talk or text with a trained counselor or advocate who can help you find resources. There are also many support groups that spring up organically on social media sites. These can be great resources for some people, but I would caution you to be careful when you enter a new group. Social media groups are often run by amateurs without any clinical experience and may be full of people who still have a lot of work to do on their recovery. They will likely not offer expert advice. Additionally, you can't always verify whom you are speaking to on social media, so be careful about opening up about your personal stuff in a group you don't know and trust. For all of these reasons, it's much better to join a group hosted by a trusted clinic or organization if you can. If you have a therapist or counselor, ask them if they know of local organizations that host support groups in your area.

For those of us in addiction recovery, Twelve Step recovery meetings are everywhere. There are meetings happening all over the world every hour on the hour. Finding the right one is the trick. There are many meetings that cater to specific populations to allow for safer or easier sharing, such as women-only meetings, LGBTQ-specific meetings, meetings for young people, meetings for atheists and agnostics, meetings conducted in Spanish, and more. If you've tried the Twelve Steps and know it's not the right program for you, there are a growing number of organizations providing alternatives. SMART Recovery is one other popular organization that offers meetings rooted in cognitive-behavioral therapy.

. . .

It's important to recognize that everyone is at a different place in their healing journey, and everyone has different needs. Perhaps just reading this book may be enough for you to construct a process of recovery that works for you. Maybe your most pressing need is to find a good counselor or therapist who understands sexual trauma. Or maybe finding a community of survivors with different perspectives whom you can talk with daily is the element your recovery is missing. Everyone's needs are unique to them, and we should never judge anyone for what they need to get through the day. Some people need to go to a support group or meeting every day, while others may go once a month or stop going after a period of time. The most important thing is to find what works for you. Commonly, more supports are required at the beginning of your healing in order for you to learn the coping skills and find the resources available to help you stabilize. After some months or years, many people feel stable enough to stop attending support meetings or stop going to therapy. I would urge you to keep at least a couple people or resources at the ready even in long-term recovery for those times when an unexpected loss, change, or triggering situation comes up in your life. Otherwise, do whatever works for you.

Finding your community, whether that be one close person, a small group, or a large online network, can help give you a sense of purpose. For many survivors, getting involved in advocacy is an important part of healing. Many sexual assault organizations and victim service agencies are led and staffed by survivors who once needed these services. Survivors make amazing advocates, policy makers, nonprofit leaders, community organizers, and more. We need places of power and influence to be filled with the voices of those who have personal experience with the issues and understand what's needed on a fundamental level. We have seen the evidence of the power of survivors joined together in the #MeToo and Time's Up movements and their actions across the United States and the world. Survivors are storming their respective capitol buildings and demanding policy change, and amazing connections are being made all over the world. There are events, rallies, town hall meetings, and communities waiting to accept you with open arms. You just have to look around. If you live in a remote or rural area without access to many resources near you, the internet holds a wealth of information and opportunities to lend your virtual voice. If you do not have access to the internet at home, try your local library for free computer and internet access, books, and news about what may be happening in your community.

If you're thinking about getting involved in advocacy, I would encourage you to try it—we need you. The best way to start is to reach out to your local rape crisis center or victim service organization and ask about volunteering. Many survivors start their own groups, whether that be out of a lack of resources in their own community or a dissatisfaction with the level of service they did or did not receive in their community. That's okay too. The more support we have in this world for survivors, the better. I will offer one note of caution: when you put yourself out there, when you share your story, others will find you. This is amazingly fulfilling in and of itself. It can also be challenging. You may be the only person that other person has ever connected with. You may be the first person they have ever opened up to, and you could wind up getting inundated with emotional responses, requests, and responsibilities. I want you to know this: You cannot save everyone. You cannot help every other survivor.

I learned this the hard way. When I started speaking out over twenty years ago, there were very few survivors doing so. I would often be the first person someone had heard giving voice to their feelings and experiences, and both my heart and my in-box filled with the newly disclosed stories of survivors. I took the responsibility of being these survivors' first confidant very seriously. I still do. What I did not understand back then is the importance of boundaries. You have to put your own healing and peace first. You may have heard the saying "If your own house is not in order, you cannot bring order to anyone else's." That's so true.

I've watched other survivors abandon their own healing to try to save everyone who comes across their path. I have watched them suffer in this valiant attempt. Helping others is important and can be very healing. But I need you to hear me clearly on this. Healing someone else is *not your job. You cannot save everyone.* The only person you are responsible for today is *you.* Even if you're an advocate or a therapist yourself, you have to set boundaries. You do your job listening and dispensing wisdom when you're on the clock, and then you have to stop and fill up your own cup. Organize your own inner house. Your healing, your emotional well-being, must always come first.

There's a reason you have to place the air mask on yourself first on an airplane—you cannot help the person next to you if you are denying yourself oxygen. You will both die. Your healing and recovery are exactly the same. You can give resources. You can lend your experience. And then you must step back and allow that survivor to pave their own path toward healing. You cannot be a person's sole source of emotional support if

166 CHAPTER 10

it drains your own tank. If, like me, you choose to make this work your career, that's wonderful; we need you. It's a beautiful thing when two survivors find one another and can guide each other. The understanding, the unspoken communication that happens when you are with other survivors is incredible. Healing and recovery are gifts that are meant to be given away to others in need. Do this work as long as it is not done at your own expense. Understand your own limitations, put proper ethical boundaries in place, and use your own support network and resources when needed.

I'm talking so much about this balance because it can be super hard. Women especially are often expected to be emotional caregivers, and we internalize that role in unhealthy ways. Being compassionate does not mean we have to give and give until there's nothing left. In fact, that pattern can backfire and lead to burnout that prevents you from helping anyone. For too many years, I made myself accessible to all survivors at all times, at all costs. It almost took me out at times. There were times when I was so emotionally depleted that all my boundaries were blurred, and I was anxiety ridden all the time. If my phone buzzed, I was immediately there trying to save whoever needed me. I discovered the hard way that this can be a recipe for disaster. I never relapsed or fell back into addictive behaviors, but I will tell you there were times I was not emotionally well. I was not my best self, and I had the potential to do harm to everyone around me because I was not taking proper care of myself. Today, I keep my boundaries clear. I resource people. I try not to confuse my work with my personal life. I have an automatic message on my social media that lets people know that I cannot always respond right away, but there are many hotlines and organizations they can contact who can. I offer support and guidance, but I gently let people know that I am not a therapist and that they will need to find someone else to be a daily contact for them. I plant the seeds and let others do their own growing. This allows me the space and energy to get up and do the advocacy that I do each day while safeguarding my own healing and recovery.

Do I have perfectly clear boundaries at all times? No. A big chunk of my personal community is made up of folks whom I met through my work. That will naturally happen. You will meet people through the course of this work with whom you will have strong connections. If you are in the trenches long enough, you will form a bond with some people that is unbreakable. You will develop friendships with people out of common struggles.

· · ·

Your voice, your choice to live your truth out loud, may also cost you people. Some people cannot handle the reality that comes with our circumstances. Hear me clearly: those are not your fucking people. Okay? Lately we've become unfortunately aware of some of the dangers that can come from speaking out about your experience with sexual violence. Sometimes when survivors come forward in the media, they get slayed. With the advent of social media, this experience is worse than ever before. In the past, when we needed a break from ignorant people's comments, we could turn off the TV, take the phone off the hook, and throw away the paper. It's much harder when the device in your hand continues to buzz with social media updates. We have seen survivors go through emotional hell online by having their names, their stories, and the details of their cases dissected by trolls online. Everyone is an armchair journalist these days; everyone has a blog and an opinion, and they aren't afraid to give it. When we speak our truth or dare to publicly support others who are telling their truth, we can become subject to ridicule.

There are still far too many people in our society who don't want to believe survivors. Some of these people are offenders themselves and therefore want to make sure no one speaks out about them. Other times, these people are just ignorant about the reality of what we have gone through and don't realize how hurtful they are being. The scope of the #MeToo movement has also led to a lot of fatigue and backlash. People have had to contend with the reality that some of their heroes, friends, family, favorite actors, producers, coaches, and priests are perpetrators of horrible crimes. Secrets and rumors are now hashtags, and it has been overwhelming for everyone.

On the one hand, it has been incredibly freeing and validating to watch offenders finally be held accountable and to see so many survivors find their voice and speak their truth. But it has also ripped open emotional wounds all over the world and has torn apart entire families, organizations, and institutions. It should be no surprise that some people just want to put their heads back into the sand and not listen to it anymore. It's emotional. It's horrific, and it's heartbreaking. While we have seen more support for survivors than ever before, there is still so much work to be done. So much awareness. So much needed dialogue.

After the death of Kobe Bryant in January 2020, many women, reporters, and survivors started speaking in the media about the rape allegation against him from earlier in his career. We saw the media exploit people who were attempting to engage in a conversation while others were vilified for it. A *Washington Post* reporter was put on leave for even mentioning it online, and Gayle King received death threats for asking a female athlete about it. Considering Bryant was a hero to so many young people and athletes, it was a very confusing and emotional situation for many. And as it becomes more and more acceptable to have these discussions in public spaces, we will encounter many messy situations like this. We still have a lot of work to do on learning the best ways to engage with these topics while also protecting the victims involved. We have a lot of healing to do, both as individuals and as a society.

As survivors at this moment, we have to gauge our own spiritual fitness before we wade into these very public waters of debate. I am an aggressive advocate, and I will often call people out for bad behavior. I have found that social media is not always the safest or most constructive way one can do this. I have to determine my audience and my impact. Am I just going to be joining a chorus of screaming people and get attacked? Or does my voice, my tweet, my update have the ability to move the conversation in a productive way? And can I send it and disengage from the negativity that will most likely accompany the likes, shares, and support? Being able to separate out the trolls from those who truly need to hear your story, your words, and your take on a situation is important if you are going to engage these conversations in public ways. At the end of the day, not everyone will like you, not everyone will agree with your point of view, and not everyone will be a part of your support circle. And honestly, that's probably for the best.

I have grown enough in my life to know that a small handful of people who truly get me are better than an address book full of fake friends. I have no time for people who refuse to understand me, so I have had to eliminate certain people from my world. This can be painful as hell. It's hard to cut the cord on attachments that no longer serve us. But it is necessary for our own well-being. Find people who welcome your broken parts. Find people who understand and appreciate all of you, not just the best parts of you. If someone doesn't want to look at you for who you really are, then they are not worth your time. There are so many others out there who will see you and welcome you. People who will not just look at you but mirror back more compassion, love, and understanding than you can imagine. Find those people.

EXERCISE

What type of people or community do you need in your life? I've found that I need different kinds of support at different times. For me, my supports tend to fall into these buckets:

- *Emotional support:* people I can lean on, get a hug from, talk to while knowing I will get unconditional love in return
- *Distraction support:* people I can just laugh with, share stupid jokes with, or call to go to a movie or on a hike
- *Guidance support:* people who can offer me resources or solid ideas on what to do next
- *Recovery support:* people in support groups, my therapist, or others who will take me to a meeting or whom I can call to talk about my recovery from addiction or sexual trauma

These are vital kinds of support for my ongoing recovery and healing. In your journal, try to identify what your needs are. You can use my categories or define your own. List the people who currently fall into each bucket for you. For each person, list how you will contact them if you need that kind of support. If you can't think of anyone who could give you a kind of support you need, make a plan on how to meet new people who could help you.

Meditation

Today, I don't have to settle for people who do not understand my struggles. I can seek and find new connections. I will honor myself enough to know I deserve these connections.

Mantra

The only person I can focus on is myself. While my story may guide another toward healing of their own, their healing is not mine.

11

Setback or Feedback

*I now know that I have a purpose in life, and as long as I
continue to live an open and honest life, I will continue to
cherish that gift. I don't always do it perfectly, but that is not
the point. It is about progress and living along a spiritual
path of continual growth. I try to look at everything as a
learning experience and a way for me to personally grow.*

—BLACKOUT GIRL, PAGES 237–238

YOU ARE NOT PERFECT. I know, this may come as a shock
to you, but you aren't, and neither am I. We are going to make
mistakes. Shit, we *have* to make mistakes. That's how we learn.
It's how we grow. People often ask me how I have gotten this
far without relapsing. How have I gotten to this place in my life
without running back to my old habits? My response is that it's
not worth it for me today. That could very well change tomorrow.
I hope not. I'm pretty sure it won't, but none of us is immune to
falling back. I'm not arrogant enough to think that I'm above any
of the behaviors that could lead me back down a dark path.

What gives me hope and strength is that I have different
skills today than I did five, ten, or twenty years ago. Everything
I've experienced and learned so far decreases the likelihood of
me using drugs and alcohol today. My recovery has always been

about making daily choices that keep me on a path of healing and recovery. I'm not coasting—I'm constantly aware that I'm not perfect, and I'm working on those imperfect parts of myself all the time. That is where my hard work lies. Am I being helpful or hurtful? Am I being honest just to make a point or to truly benefit someone? Am I being an asshole? Have I made amends when I was an asshole? The way I approach my life today is that everything is a lesson. Every situation, success, setback, or mistake I have in my life offers a moment where I can pause and evaluate what it all means.

Let me be really clear about something: recovery from both addiction and sexual trauma is *hard*. It is not for the faint of heart. Diving deep into your past and bringing forth all your baggage is the work of warriors. It's messy. It's ugly at times. And at other times it's utterly, beautifully freeing. But it is not a linear path; there will be so many twists and turns in your journey. Some turns will take you to unexpected places that unearth new truths and allow you to breathe deeper. Others will make you feel like you are choking and may never breathe free again. I promise that you will.

Life on life's terms is messy. Dealing with our shit is messy. There will be times when you will doubt everything. Where you will cease to see all the progress you made and slide back into shame and self-loathing. That is normal. It is temporary. I promise you. There will also be times when you are on the top of the world and feeling completely invincible. Neither of these extremes is where the real growth happens. The challenge is figuring out how to bring yourself back into balance. There's a reason we tend to value the extreme moments in life. Living like you're on top of the world with no worries is easier. It feels safer. But for us, extremes can be dangerous. It's important to understand that we are just as vulnerable to relapsing or engaging in bad decisions whether we are flying high or at rock bottom. Many think you are susceptible only when you are low—that's not accurate. We have to be ever vigilant about our recovery and anything that may threaten it.

This next part is really important. Sometimes we do everything "right." We learn and grow and use all the tools at our disposal to keep our recovery solid, and we still fall back. Relapse happens. Whether it be a relapse to past emotional patterns, an unhealthy relationship, or drinking and drugging, it is not the end of the world. You are not these mistakes. They will not and do not define you. Relapse is not failure—it is feedback. It doesn't mean that you are back at ground zero. It doesn't erase any of your past successes. It simply means there is more work to do, more inside you to uncover and move through. That is all. A relapse can be your body's and mind's way of getting your attention and helping you better understand yourself.

Life is a journey, not a destination. I know that's cliché as fuck, but in this case, it really is true. There's no final destination to life on this earth. Maybe you believe in an afterlife; maybe you don't. Either way, as long as we're here on this planet, we are going to keep living. We are going to keep traveling, meeting new people, discovering new things about ourselves, engaging in new work, losing people we love, having painful experiences, feeling explosions of joy, and so much more. I have had amazing experiences so far in recovery. All I have to do is look down at my wrists to remember that there was a time when I didn't think my life was worth living. That past version of myself had no idea what was to come. Since then, I've experienced happiness and joy at levels I never knew were possible. I have also made mistakes that hurt people, including myself. They have all been valuable gifts. They all taught me something about myself and where I was in those moments.

If you can be open to the constant process of self-discovery, you will be able to get through all of it. The good and the bad.

There are still times I find myself retreating deep into the recesses of my mind, into the dark places where no one can find me, and I simmer there. There is this odd degree of comfort there, like an old friend, a warm blanket. I honor those spaces today because I know they will never fully go away. For me, it's about diving deep into that abyss, swimming around in it, and asking myself, "What am I seeking here?" Am I avoiding something in my life? Am I on the brink of a bad decision? If the answer is yes, I have to tell myself to *get out*. My head can be a dangerous place. But I don't fear it anymore. When I find myself drawn to a dark emotional place, I no longer immediately label myself as a freak or sick. I don't shame myself anymore. I know it's there, it's a part of me, and lingering there sometimes may allow me to learn something new about myself or my situation.

This is the reality of being a survivor and a person in recovery. We all have darkness inside us that will always be there to some degree. For me, maybe it's the root of my addiction, or maybe it's the storage area for all the pain I experienced as a child. Whatever it is, it is part of me. What I do have to be careful of when exploring my dark places is self-sabotage. Self-sabotage is behavior that leads you backward, and it's very common for us. It's the noise in our head, the negative talk that happens in the recesses of our mind that tries to convince us to engage in behaviors that are not healthy for us. This is usually rooted in our self-esteem. It also often happens when we're living in one of the extremes I mentioned earlier.

Self-sabotage might come in the form of the thoughts in your head that say, "Well, I already failed. I might as well [insert unhealthy behavior here]." The voices in your head tell you that you are already worthless, so why not do that other thing? For example: You are having a bad day and feeling horrible about yourself. You walk into the break room at work and see they are having a luncheon for someone's birthday. So you drown your sorrows in some pepperoni pizza, even though you know it may make you sick or lead to an unhealthy pattern of behavior. Then the voices in your head start. "Ugh, why did I eat this pizza? I'm a bad person. Fuck it, give me another slice! Now I really did it. Ugh, I'm so mad at myself, but since I am already here, yes, give me all the cake." And by the time you are done, you're sitting with a pile of calories, a stomachache, some gas, and a side of self-loathing. This is what I call a "pile-on mentality," and it's a common way we self-sabotage.

But, this doesn't happen only when we're already feeling low. We're also at risk of self-sabotage when we are feeling too good about ourselves, when we're all wrapped up in our egos. It could look like this: "Man, do I feel great. I have worked out every night this week. I have food-prepped every day and avoided everything that may make me sick. I deserve something sweet. Shit, I earned something sweet. Surely I've worked out enough to negate any impact of a piece of cake." You walk into the same break room, and three pieces of cake, five handfuls of chips, and two slices of pizza later, you're no longer feeling great and are wondering what happened.

Both scenarios end the same. This could apply to anything that you have used as an unhealthy coping mechanism: drinking, smoking, sex, food, shopping. In those moments, our job is to take a step back and appreciate what's happening. In both instances, we let ourselves revel in extreme emotional states, and it resulted in self-sabotage. It's in that awareness, in our ability to step back and observe ourselves and notice the connections between our behaviors, where the most growth can occur. Sometimes we are able to do this right in the moment and stop ourselves from making mistakes. Sometimes we may have to fall down and spend a bit of time lying among the ruins before we determine what happened. Self-reflection is one of our most powerful tools in recovery. Use it to see and learn the lessons from your missteps.

This is the "how" of living a life free from our addictions. It is not about being perfect and avoiding all mistakes; it's about being healthy enough to walk through those mistakes with grace and see the lesson waiting on the other side. You come out wiser, and you come out stronger. It takes a lot of work to get to this point. You have to do the massive overhaul that we've already talked about, the unearthing of all the old stuff in order to make room for the new stuff. Once that room is made, though, you will find that your life is full of joy, peace, and freedom. That does not mean you will stop experiencing pain, loss, and hurt. It just means that you now have room to deal with it in a way that is less harmful to you and others. You have cleared a path for it and formed a plan, so when it comes into your world, it should not overwhelm you to the point that you wind up back where you were. If and when something happens that throws you way off course, use the tools you learned in this book to work through your healing process. Acknowledge the feelings you need to experience, fully engage them, and allow yourself the beautiful gift of being human. I have found proof in my own recovery that this works. Because I did the hard work of creating space in my life, these moments, life events, and struggles are less painful than they were when I still had all that past suffering stored up inside me. You are worth those lessons.

· · ·

Think back to science class, when you learned about homeostasis. Our bodies are always trying to achieve chemical balance. For me, recovery is the emotional equivalent. If I live in the extremes, if I live out on the edges, then I am shifted spiritually, emotionally, and mentally into a space that does not fully serve me.

Your whole center of gravity is thrown off balance when you are on the edge. Sometimes, all you can see is the cliff. When you take a step back and move into the middle, your perspective can expand and take in all that is around you. Yes, the cliff is still there, but there are also beautiful trees ahead, the sun bursting through the clouds, birds flying free above you.

There is so much strength in your tears, fears, and struggle. Please do not let anyone else tell you differently. The things about us that others often perceive as weaknesses arc actually signs of our strength. If you own your mistakes, use your voice, strive for daily compassion and balance, and are committed to learning and growth, you are magic. To me, you are a superhero for doing this work. The only true mistakes in your life are those moments when you did not try, you did not get back up, or you did not want to make things right. Once you realize that, you will begin to understand that nothing is beyond your reach. Everything is possible, and you are the only one standing in the way of you. Do not underestimate your own power and worth. Do the thing that scares you. Dream big. Be brave in your explorations and know that even if you don't reach your original goal, you will gain something. Maybe that something is just the ability to say, "Hey, I tried that, and it didn't work out. Now I know." There is so much growth in that. Do not limit yourself, and please, never give up on you. You are worth the work.

People ask me all the time, "How did you do it?" How did I survive it all, and how do I stay clean and sober? My single greatest tool is my self-awareness. You now have all of my so-called secrets. I hope this book has given you the tools necessary to take a similar journey with yourself. The time and effort are so worth the reward. I want to leave you with what that looks like for me today, just the start of an average day in my life.

. . .

I wake up to a surge of energy rushing through my veins. My mind immediately begins to spin as I think of everything I want to do today. I turn to my wife and rattle off five very different goals. I am pinging from one to another when she stops me ever so gently, looks at me, and says, "Baby, get on the bike. You're spinning."

Now, confronted with my current condition, I could easily bite her fucking head off (old me), or I can take a look at myself and lean into the beauty of this moment. This other human gets me. I have someone in my life who wants me to be the best version of myself. She is not judging me with her gentle nudge; she is loving me in a way very few can or know how to. Healthy me welcomes this and knows this is exactly what I need.

I smile and jump onto the bike. I start an '80s rock ride because I know the energy coursing through me right now needs a hard-core release. I need to scream, pound the pedals, and push myself beyond my comfort zone to get this shit out of my body, mind, and spirit. This energetic release is what I require to not fall back into a lesser version of myself. This thirty-minute workout is all that stands in the way of the day I want. Will I release this extra stored energy and give it a proper, healthy outlet? Or will I refuse, be mad at my wife, blame her for my current angst, and proceed to spew this energy onto undeserving people throughout my day? Will I surrender to what I have learned about myself, as a growing yet imperfect human being? That is my choice today and every day. It is also your choice, my friend, my soul companion on this journey of healing. You have the power to choose. Choose wisely, my friend, because your life literally depends upon it.

EXERCISE

Spend some time writing in your journal about why you are worth this work, why you deserve healing. Write about everything you have accomplished already and everything you hope to accomplish in the future. Write about everything that makes you kind, beautiful, compassionate, strong, intelligent, or creative. What good things have other people said about you recently? The next time your self-worth is low, return to this page and read what you wrote.

Meditation

Today and every day, I will seek to understand myself and embrace the lessons around me. I will not judge the fall; I will embrace the standing up.

Mantra

I am worth the work. I am a fucking superhero.

Resources

HEALING FROM BOTH ADDICTION AND TRAUMA are *hard work*. None of us can do it alone or without support systems. Here are some good resources that you may want to check out on your road to recovery.

Do you need help with your addiction recovery?
There are so many resources and places to get help, and they are all at your fingertips. Here are but a few of them:

> Try **Alcoholics Anonymous**: www.aa.org
> Or **Narcotics Anonymous**: www.na.org
>
> If you know the Twelve Steps don't work for you, you can try **SMART Recovery**: www.smartrecovery.org
>
> To get your questions about addiction and treatment answered, call the national helpline for the **Substance Abuse and Mental Health Services Administration**: 800-662-4357

Addiction often runs in families. If you think a loved one has a drinking or drug problem and it is affecting your life, there are groups to help you with that too. Try one of these:

Al-Anon helps family and friends who are worried about a loved one's drinking.
https://al-anon.org

Alateen, a subset of Al-Anon, is specifically for teens dealing with an alcoholic loved one.
https://al-anon.org/al-anon-meetings/find-an-alateen-meeting/

If your parent is the one with a drinking problem or another dysfunctional behavior, an Adult Children of Alcoholics meeting may be right for you.
https://adultchildren.org

Nar-Anon Family Groups support people with a loved one who is using drugs.
www.nar-anon.org

If you're looking for an alternative to the Twelve Steps, SMART Recovery also offers Family and Friends meetings.
www.smartrecovery.org/family/

People at these organizations are always there waiting to listen to you and help you. They'll even pick you up and take you to a meeting.

If you are looking for an addiction treatment center, try the Hazelden Betty Ford Foundation. Since 1949, staff have helped people reclaim their lives from the disease of addiction by using a variety of evidence-based

therapeutic approaches. Hazelden Betty Ford offers treatment for both youth and adults as well as a three-day family program for the loved ones of those seeking treatment. It is a wonderful comprehensive center, but if it isn't right for you, the experts there can direct you to other resources or other centers.
www.hazeldenbettyford.org

Do you think you may have an eating disorder?
Just like any other disease, if left untreated, an eating disorder can lead to all kinds of problems, like liver damage, throat damage, and possibly death.

The **National Eating Disorders Association** has great resources, and you can call its toll-free helpline to talk to someone in confidence.
www.nationaleatingdisorders.org
800-931-2237

Are you or a friend having suicidal thoughts?
Suicide is no joke. If you are having these thoughts or you have a friend or loved one who has expressed these thoughts, contact these organizations for help. Sometimes it is scary and hard to think about reaching out to someone who knows us or the people in our lives. That is why hotlines like these are available. They are free and confidential. You don't have to suffer in silence; there is help.

Crisis Text Line
If you are in crisis, reach out for help 24/7.
Text HOME to 741741.
www.crisistextline.org

National Suicide Prevention Lifeline
800-273-TALK (800-273-8255)
www.suicidepreventionlifeline.org

Are you a victim of a crime?
As I've mentioned in this book, you have many rights under the law. You have the right to be heard in the criminal justice process, to receive restitution, to be present at your trial or hearing, and to be treated with dignity, compassion, and respect. You also have rights to compensation, to protection, to a speedy trial, and to information about the status of your case. To learn more about your rights as a crime victim, check out these resources:

The National Center for Victims of Crime
www.victimsofcrime.org

Office for Victims of Crime
www.ovc.gov

Rape, Abuse & Incest National Network
The Rape, Abuse & Incest National Network offers help that's free, confidential, and also available 24/7 through its National Sexual Assault Hotline.
www.rainn.org
800-656-HOPE (4673)

If you are a male survivor, **1 in 6** is a resource to find support specific to your needs. They offer a 24/7 online chat helpline.
www.1in6.org

The **"Me Too" Movement** website, sponsored by the New York nonprofit Girls for Gender Equity, contains a library of resources for sexual assault and abuse survivors and their allies.
https://metoomvmt.org/healing-resources-library

Are you wondering whether you are gay or trans?
Whether you are just questioning your sexuality or identity or you know for certain that you are LGBTQ, it is helpful to reach out and find support. Things are so much better today for queer youth and adults, but there are still many challenges, fears, acts of discrimination, and much hatred in this world. The goal is to keep you safe and to help you find an environment that will foster healthy questioning and development. Here are some places to look for help:

GLSEN (Gay, Lesbian, and Straight Education Network)
www.glsen.org

Human Rights Campaign
www.hrc.org

National LGBTQ Task Force
www.thetaskforce.org

National Center for Transgender Equality
www.nctequality.org

The Trevor Project
The Trevor Project is a judgment-free resource for LGBTQ youth who are in crisis or struggling with suicidal thoughts. Call the TrevorLifeline at 866-488-7386, text START to 678678, or visit www.thetrevorproject.org to find more resources.

Do you need more help processing your trauma or another mental health disorder?

I firmly believe that those of us who have experienced deep emotional, psychological, or physical harm must find a trained, licensed, trauma-informed therapist to help us work through our healing process. The organizations and resources below can help you learn more about the various programs and therapies that are proven to work.

The **National Child Traumatic Stress Network (NCTSN)** was created by Congress in 2000 as part of the Children's Health Act to raise the standard of care and increase access to services for children and families who experience or witness traumatic events. www.nctsn.org

The **Trauma Center,** part of the Justice Resource Institute, has a library of resources for people dealing with many different types of trauma. www.traumacenter.org

Substance Abuse and Mental Health Services Administration (SAMHSA) has resources on its webpage to help you cope with all kinds of behavioral health issues. www.samhsa.gov

National Alliance on Mental Illness (NAMI) provides valuable resources on coping with all kinds of mental health issues, including support groups for people with mental health disorders and their families. NAMI Helpline: 800-950-NAMI or text NAMI to 741741 www.nami.org

Here are some other resources that helped me cope with the aftermath of sexual assault and addiction:

Insight Timer: Insight Timer is an app that can be downloaded onto any mobile device. It contains thousands of meditations, mantras, talks, guided meditations, and music tracks to help calm, soothe, and restore the mind and spirit. I use the app often.

Eye Movement Desensitization and Reprocessing (EMDR) music stimulates both the right and left sides of the brain to promote harmony. It's helpful for times of extreme stress and anxiety. For me, it calms the little storms that can brew in my brain and allows me to focus and breathe better. You can find EMDR music in the Insight Timer app, on other music purchasing apps, or on YouTube.

Are you a teenager struggling with sexual trauma and addiction? Many of the resources listed above may be helpful for you, so be sure to look into them.

Another great source of free information is your local public library. Librarians are trained to be nonjudgmental and to put patron privacy first. Many libraries also now have self-checkout stations so you can check out materials without having to talk with any staff.

Above all, remember that you are not alone, and the traumas you may have endured are not your fault.

Are you a parent who is worried about your adolescent child?
Trying to parent a child who is struggling with any of the above issues can be a thoroughly exhausting and heartbreaking ordeal. Many of the resources listed above can help parents find support for themselves as well as better understand and help their children. I also highly recommend that you seek out your own trauma-informed therapist. Whether or not you have experienced issues similar to those your child is experiencing, talking with a trained therapist can help you process your feelings as a parent and find healing for yourself and your family. In addition, you may want to use the following:

> The **American Academy of Child & Adolescent Psychiatry** is a great resource for parents to educate themselves and find help.
> www.aacap.org

> There are now several groups specifically designed to support parents struggling with a child's addiction, including the closed Facebook support group **The Addict's Mom** and the website **MomPower.org**.

I hope you find these resources helpful. Please know there is no shame in seeking help. The people at these organizations are there especially for you. Life is hard, and we go through so many ups and downs. Here is one certainty I can offer you as the best resource possible: *you never have to go through anything alone again.* Reach out, ask for help, and try something, anything healthy, that will help ease your pain or answer your questions.

With much love and respect,
Jennifer Storm

Professional Resources

Healing Trauma, Second Edition
STEPHANIE COVINGTON, PHD
Introducing *Healing Trauma,* an evidence-based, gender-responsive, six-session (90-minute sessions) curriculum for women, designed for settings in which a short-term intervention is needed. Visit Hazelden. org/store to learn more, download the Scope and Sequence, see sample chapters, and watch a video featuring author Stephanie Covington, PhD.

Beyond Trauma, Second Edition
STEPHANIE COVINGTON, PHD
Beyond Trauma: A Healing Journey for Women is an evidence-based, twelve-session curriculum designed to help women and girls recover from the effects of trauma in their lives. Visit Hazelden.org/store to learn more, download the Scope and Sequence, see sample chapters, and watch a video featuring author Stephanie Covington, PhD.

Moving from Trauma-Informed to Trauma-Responsive
STEPHANIE COVINGTON, PHD
Becoming trauma-responsive means looking at all aspects of an organization's programming, environment, language, and values and involving all staff in better serving clients who have experienced trauma. *Moving from Trauma-Informed to Trauma-Responsive* provides program administrators and clinical directors with all the resources needed to train staff and make organizational changes to become trauma-responsive. This comprehensive training program involves all staff, ensuring clients are served with a trauma-responsive approach at every interaction. Developed by leading trauma experts Stephanie S. Covington, PhD, and Sandra L. Bloom, MD.

Notes

1. Substance Abuse and Mental Health Services Administration, *Key Substance Use and Mental Health Indicators in the United States: Results from the 2017 National Survey on Drug Use and Health* (HHS Publication No. SMA 18-5068, NSDUH Series H-53), Rockville, MD: Center for Behavioral Health Statistics and Quality, Substance Abuse and Mental Health Services Administration (2018), https://www.samhsa.gov/data/report/2017-nsduh-annual-national-report.

2. R. E. Morgan and B. A. Oudekerk, *Criminal Victimization, 2018*, Bureau of Justice Statistics, National Crime Victimization Survey 2018 (September 2019), https://www.bjs.gov/content/pub/pdf/cv18.pdf.

3. S. G. Smith, X. Zhang, K. C. Basile, M. T. Merrick, J. Wang, M. Kresnow, and J. Chen, *The National Intimate Partner and Sexual Violence Survey: 2015 Data Brief—Updated Release*, Centers for Disease Control and Prevention (November 2018), https://www.cdc.gov/violenceprevention/pdf/2015 data-brief508.pdf.

4. H. N. Snyder, "Sexual Assault of Young Children as Reported to Law Enforcement: Victim, Incident, and Offender Characteristics," Bureau of Justice Statistics (July 2000).

5. W. R. Corbin, J. A. Bernat, K. S. Calhoun, L. D. McNair, and K. L. Seals, "Role of Alcohol Expectancies and Alcohol Consumption Among Sexually Victimized and Nonvictimized College Women," *Journal of Interpersonal Violence* 16, no. 4 (April 1, 2001): 297–311, https://doi.org/10.1177 /088626001016004002.

6. National Center on Substance Abuse and Child Welfare, "Trauma-Informed Care," https://ncsacw.samhsa.gov/resources /trauma/default.aspx.

7. RAINN (Rape, Abuse & Incest National Network), "Victims of Sexual Violence: Statistics," https://www.rainn.org/statistics /victims-sexual-violence.

8. C. Vendel, "Man Will Spend Up to 40 Years in Prison for Raping Woman He Followed from Downtown Harrisburg Bar," PennLive *Patriot-News*, updated October 18, 2019, https://www .pennlive.com/news/2019/10/man-will-spend-up-to-40-years -in-prison-for-raping-woman-he-followed-from-downtown -harrisburg-bar.html.

9. S. Cottrell, "How Mommy Drinking Culture Has Normalized Alcoholism for Women in America," Babysitter Mom, https:// babysittermom.com/how-mommy-drinking-culture-has -normalized-alcoholism-for-women-in-america/. Originally published on the Disney blog Babble.

10. J. Liebschutz, J. B. Savetsky, R. Saitz, N. J. Horton, C. Lloyd-Travaglini, and J. H. Samet, "The Relationship between Sexual and Physical Abuse and Substance Abuse Consequences," *Journal of Substance Abuse Treatment* 22, no. 3 (April 1, 2002): 121–28, https://doi.org/10.1016/S0740-5472(02)00220-9.

11. National Sexual Violence Resource Center, "Statistics," https://www.nsvrc.org/node/4737.

12. Centers for Disease Control and Prevention, "The National Intimate Partner and Sexual Violence Survey: An Overview of 2010 Findings on Victimization by Sexual Orientation," https://www.cdc.gov/violenceprevention/pdf/cdc_nisvs_victimization_final-a.pdf; S. E. James, J. L. Herman, S. Rankin, M. Keisling, L. Mottet, and M. Anafi, *The Report of the 2015 U.S. Transgender Survey* (Washington, DC: National Center for Transgender Equality, 2016), https://www.transequality.org/sites/default/files/docs/USTS-Full-Report-FINAL.PDF.

13. National Institutes of Health, "Alcohol-Related Deaths Increasing in the United States," January 10, 2020, https://www.nih.gov/news-events/news-releases/alcohol-related-deaths-increasing-united-states.

14. L. M. Hartling, W. Rosen, M. Walker, and J. V. Jordan, "Shame and Humiliation: From Isolation to Relational Transformation," *Work in Progress* 88, Wellesley Centers for Women, Wellesley College (2000), http://www.humiliationstudies.org/documents/hartling/HartlingShameHumiliation.pdf.

15. L. Hawks, S. Woolhandler, D. U. Himmelstein, D. H. Bor, A. Gaffney, and D. McCormick, "Association between Forced Sexual Initiation and Health Outcomes Among US Women," *JAMA Internal Medicine* 179, no. 11 (September 16, 2019): 1551–58, https://doi.org/10.1001/jamainternmed.2019.3500.

16. K. B. Wolitzky-Taylor, H. S. Resnick, A. B. Amstadter, J. L. McCauley, K. J. Ruggiero, and D. G. Kilpatrick, "Reporting Rape in a National Sample of College Women," *Journal of American College Health* 59, no. 7 (2011): 582–87, https://doi.org/10.1080/07448481.2010.515634.

Acknowledgments

I wish to thank my father, who provided me with unconditional love and support. You are my hero in heaven. To my stepmother, who has been an angel to me and in many ways saved me, I cherish and love you. To my brothers, Brian and Jimi, for providing me with constant laughter and unconditional love and support. I love you both so much. You are such a blessing in my life. To my niece, Cheyanne, who serves as the other daily reflection of me. You are my angel eyes; I adore you! To Parker, my beautiful nephling whose struggles reflect my own in so many ways, may you find your path and blaze it powerfully. To my son, Victor, who makes me laugh every day and challenges me in ways I never knew possible. When you slip your hand into mine, the world disappears and my heart melts.

To the love of my life and my wife, Fianne. Your tolerance, support, boundless energy, and endless love for me is something I never thought I would find. You ground me, you lift me up, and my life has been forever changed by your love.

To Phyllis Parsons, my manager and dear friend, for always believing in my story and my strength. To all the editors and staff at Hazelden: thank you for believing in my story and experiences enough to share them with the world. To all my friends and fellow people in recovery and survivors whom I have met along this amazing journey—you have each touched my life in very special ways. I am eternally grateful to each and every one of you. I have learned so much through my interactions with each of you. I carry a piece of those experiences with me daily, and they are interwoven into the very fabric of who I am today. Thank you, and peace be with you.

About the Author

Jennifer Storm is a survivor, author, advocate, and internationally recognized victims' rights expert with more than twenty years of experience. Storm has worked many high-profile cases, including helping victims of Jerry Sandusky, Bill Cosby, Catholic clergy, and thousands of others. She serves as a content expert on victims' rights in the media and tours the country sharing her experiences, including frequent live and taped appearances on all major networks. Storm has four additional publications: *Blackout Girl: Tracing My Scars from Addiction and Sexual Assault, Leave the Light On: A Memoir of Recovery and Self-Discovery, Picking Up the Pieces without Picking Up,* and *Echoes of Penn State.* She is also working on a documentary based on *Blackout Girl* to help carry the message of addiction, victimization, and trauma. Storm resides in Camp Hill, Pennsylvania, with her wife, Fianne, and their adopted son, Victor.

About Hazelden Publishing

As part of the Hazelden Betty Ford Foundation, Hazelden Publishing offers both cutting-edge educational resources and inspirational books. Our print and digital works help guide individuals in treatment and recovery, and their loved ones. Professionals who work to prevent and treat addiction also turn to Hazelden Publishing for evidence-based curricula, digital content solutions, and videos for use in schools, treatment and correctional programs, and community settings. We also offer training for implementation of our curricula.

Through published and digital works, Hazelden Publishing extends the reach of healing and hope to individuals, families, and communities affected by addiction and related issues.

For more information about Hazelden publications,
please call **800-328-9000**
or visit us online at **hazelden.org/bookstore**.

Other Titles That May Interest You

Daybreak

Meditations for Women Survivors of Sexual Abuse
MAUREEN BRADY
These 366 daily meditations extend support and wisdom to women
who have survived childhood sexual abuse.
Order No. 5053; also available as an ebook

Sane

Mental Illness, Addiction, and the Twelve Steps
MARYA HORNBACHER
In this beautifully written recovery handbook, Marya Hornbacher
applies the wisdom gained from her struggle with severe mental
illness and addiction to an honest and illuminating examination
of the challenges of working a Twelve Step program for those with
co-occurring disorders.
Order No. 3029; also available as an ebook

A Woman's Way through the Twelve Steps

BY STEPHANIE S. COVINGTON, PHD
Acknowledging that recovery raises special issues for women—from
questions about sexuality and relationships to anxieties about speaking up at mixed-gender meetings—*A Woman's Way through the Twelve
Steps* focuses directly on the feminine experience of addiction and
healing, empowering the reader to take ownership of her recovery
process as well as her growth as a woman.
Order No. 5019; also available as an ebook

Boundaries

Where You End and I Begin
ANNE KATHERINE, MA
What are boundaries and how do I set them? This deeply informative
and engaging book answers these questions and more using real-
life stories and the author's decades of professional experience as a
therapist.
Order No. 7803; also available as an ebook

Praise for *Blackout Girl*

An unvarnished, harrowing, and transformative look into the workings of trauma, and the healing, redemption, and resilience that comes from it.

—**ANDREA CONSTAND,** founder of Hope, Healing and Transformation

Storm's *Blackout Girl* cries out into the darkness that recovery from addiction and sexual assault is possible. It is a story of courage and hope.

—**CONSTANCE SCHARFF, PHD,** vice president of Rock to Recovery and addiction and mental health researcher

There is a path to recovery, even after you hit rock bottom; that you can not only heal, but use the knowledge you gained to help others, which she does.

—**NICOLE WEISENSEE EGAN,** author of *Chasing Cosby* and award-winning investigative journalist

Raw. Authentic. We are in a time of elevating consciousness, and this is the type of story the world needs to hear right now.

—**WES GEER,** former Korn guitarist and founder of Rock to Recovery

Her raw truth telling punches you in the gut, but it is her divine hope for a better tomorrow that inspires all of us to do more to help other victims and survivors.

—**KIM GOLDMAN,** victim advocate, *New York Times* best-selling author, host of *Confronting: O.J. Simpson,* and vice chair of the National Center for Victims of Crime

• • •

Since *Blackout Girl* was first published in 2008, Jennifer Storm has seen the #MeToo and Times Up movements empower countless brave survivors to reveal the truth of their experiences. More relevant than ever, Jennifer's story and professional insights expose the societal failures these victims have endured and how we can all help each other heal. Now including even more details of Jennifer's experiences and new insights on what she has learned in the past decade, this second edition of *Blackout Girl* is a must-read both for those looking to learn about the personal effects of widespread sexual assault and addiction and for those who already hold these issues dear.

Order No. 3737; also available as an ebook